The Life and Times
of

Lawman

Joe Thralls

Tom S. Coke

HERITAGE BOOKS
2008

HERITAGE BOOKS

AN IMPRINT OF HERITAGE BOOKS, INC.

Books, CDs, and more—Worldwide

For our listing of thousands of titles see our website
at
www.HeritageBooks.com

Published 2008 by
HERITAGE BOOKS, INC.
Publishing Division
100 Railroad Ave. #104
Westminster, Maryland 21157

International Standard Book Numbers
Paperbound: 978-0-7884-3561-4
Clothbound: 978-0-7884-7298-5

To

Sumner County Historical Society

To

Sumner County Historical Society

Contents

Acknowledgements

Nineteenth century Kansas newspaper articles microfilmed by Kansas State Historical Society provided much of the material found in this book. The Society has an amazing number of these papers that have proved to be a historian's gold mine.

Historian Richard L. Lane's notes in G. D. Freeman's *Midnight and Noonday* pointed the way to a number of areas worth pursuing in Joe Thralls' life. Had Lane lived to complete his work on Joe Thralls, I'm confident his work would have been far more complete than my own.

Richard M. Gilfillan, curator of the Wellington, Kansas, Chisholm Trail Museum, helped in my research. He guided me to a number of old newspapers in the basement of the museum. That's where I found the Fort Scott article of Joe Thralls' encounter with William Smith.

Old West writer and researcher Roger Myers gave me invaluable information on Thralls' family history. His articles published in Old West magazines continue to add fresh information on leading historical figures.

Donna McNeil, librarian at Wellington Carnegie Library, helped in my research on background material for this book. She and her staff aided in my research whenever needed.

Friendly lawmen at the Sumner County Sheriff's Department showed me some of their history. One wall of their office was lined with pictures of past sheriffs dating back to the nineteenth century.

The staff in the Sumner County Clerk's office gave me access to nineteenth century court cases. That's where I found much of the background on the William McDowell murder case.

Thanks go to Melvin and Della Shafer. They showed me the Thralls family gravesite.

I'm thankful for the support of my family and my in-laws: Mary and Steve White, Judy and Jim Baxter, Julie and Kevin Breshears, Lan Cao, and Christopher and Becky Coke.

My brother-in-law, Jim Baxter, keeps some of my articles on his website, 4jranch.com. And he's always ready to help in other ways.

My other brother-in-law, Steve White, has offered continuing encouragement at times I needed it most. He has helped in a number of ways to further my attempts at writing.

As always, I count most on my wife, Bobbi, for her support, which she consistently gives.

Doubtless I've left out a number of others who have helped me. Though they remain nameless, I hope they know it's my lack of memory and not their lack of help that is to blame.

Introduction

My pulse quickened as my brothers and I ran to the living room. We checked to see if our black-and-white TV was on channel 10. This happened nearly every Tuesday night at 7:30.

We watched as the screen focused on a black-dressed horseback rider. Six-shooters gleamed from his holsters. Hugh O'Brian sat straight in the saddle as the theme played.

"Wyatt Earp, Wyatt Earp, brave, courageous, and bold. Long live his fame, and long live his fortune, and long may his story be told."

A half hour later my brothers and I argued vehemently. Was Wyatt really a part of Kansas history? Or was it fairy tale stuff? (I guess my brothers and I were a little skeptical about such things). The show fascinated me. What if it were true?

Ever since then I've followed old west history, still fascinated and a bit skeptical. (Maybe that's because I grew up in Wichita, Kansas, once an Old West cow town).

The popular TV westerns died out by the 70s. But the question remains. What really happened back then?

Were there lawmen like those portrayed on TV? Were there others besides the handful mentioned in Wild West books and movies? I've since run across some that seem to come close to those images but were never included. One I've read about was Joseph M. Thralls, born 114 days after Wyatt Earp.

Joe Thralls tangled with outlaws, cowboys, and cattlemen. He dealt with horse thieves, vigilantes, and necktie parties. Records seem to indicate he often faced danger calmly.

Thralls lived in a much-traveled area of the west, near the Chisholm Trail. Many historians would contend that Texas cattle drives into Kansas and its accompanying behavior is what gave the Wild West its name.

No place played a larger role in the cattle drives and Wild West action than did Sumner County since this was where the Chisholm Trail entered Kansas. By 1871 the border town of Caldwell became the Kansas entryway. Trail drivers passed through this town as they headed north to places such as Abilene and Wichita. This enormous traffic through Sumner County continued into the middle 1870s until quarantine laws closed the trail north of Caldwell.

Even then some cattle drives continued to Caldwell before turning west to Dodge City. And when Caldwell got a railroad in 1880 it again drew an abundance of cattlemen who had their herds shipped east. So for most of the trail driving years Sumner County became well acquainted with cowboys and their behavior.

It took strong leaders to combat the wild and free action from these young cowboys. Joe Thralls, who lived in Sumner County, became one of those leaders. Few today recognize the name though he played a crucial role in taming this part of the West.

So anyone who reads about this much-publicized era should not miss the role this southern Kansas area played. They should realize that tens of thousands of Texas longhorns accompanied by hundreds of cowboys traveled through Sumner County on their way to sell their cattle. Whether they stopped at Caldwell or Hunnewell in Sumner County or continued on north to Abilene, Wichita, Ellsworth, Newton, Waterville or other less well-known places, throughout these early years, they traveled through Sumner County.

Trail drivers entering Sumner County, as mentioned, first came to Caldwell, and after 1880 possibly to Hunnewell. In the early years (1867 to 1873) they headed first to Abilene, then Wichita, Newton, or Ellsworth. Though Dodge City to the west received an increasing number of cattle in the late 1870s, some still came through Sumner County. And when a railroad cut through Sumner

2

County in 1880, Caldwell and Hunnewell took over much of the Dodge City traffic.

The cattle trade brought with it characters with money to burn, liquor to drink, guns to shoot, and women to visit. But cowboys weren't the only actors on this stage. With all the money, cattle, horses, and business going on, this couldn't help but attract a darker side. Horse and cattle thieves, train and bank robbers, claim jumpers, card sharks, and any other sort of shady characters found opportunities around them.

To control them, law abiding citizens banded together. They formed vigilante committees and posses to hunt down and hang the culprits. Eventually the legal system became more organized and played the larger role in controlling the outlaw element. This included city, township, county, and U.S. government lawmen. But it was rough going in the early years.

Admittedly writers in the past exaggerated events. Yet there was plenty of real violence and danger to lend credence to the phrase, "Wild West." And Sumner County, where hundreds of thousands of Texas cattle entered Kansas throughout these early years, was the prime example. Sumner County between 1870 and 1885 probably saw as much Wild West action as anywhere in the country.

Cattle herds from Texas reached their zenith the year Joe Thralls came to Sumner County. Cattlemen and cowboys had been trailing cattle from Texas to Kansas along the Chisholm Trail since 1867, the first year that Abilene served as a cow town. That year some 30 to 35,000 cattle passed through Sumner County on their way to Abilene. And each the following years through 1871 the number increased.

Though exact figures will never be known, estimates say the number doubled each year between 1867 and 1871. In 1868 around 60 to 70,000 passed through the county. In 1869 it jumped to 120 to 130,000. The next year saw around 250 to 300,000 and in 1871 the number was between 600 and 700,000.

One old-time settler, George Doud Freeman, moved from Augusta to Caldwell, Kansas in May 1871. Part of the way he traveled on the Chisholm Trail. On the trail between Cowskin Creek and the Ninnescah River he described the situation.

"The cattle herds were growing thicker as we [went] southward," he said. "They got so thick on the trail that there was but little room for us to use as a highway. But as we met the herds we drove around and by them the best we could, but we made very slow progress on our journey."[1]

By then some early settlers in Wichita saw the potential of a town where the cattle entered Kansas and established Caldwell. From there the trail cut through the center of the county going north and slightly east, passing a few miles west of Wellington, then left the county around Clearwater on its way to Abilene.[2]

With each herd, often numbering between 2,000 and 2,500, came a dozen or so herders or drovers. And of course these cowboys weren't the tamest of humanity. The three-quarter million cattle passing through Sumner County that year meant thousands of hurrahing cowboys came with them.

Among the wildest was 18-year-old John Wesley Hardin. In his autobiography Hardin told of some of his experiences through Kansas that year that added to his notoriety.[3]

Hardin was running from the law when he happened to go on a cattle drive that year. On his way to Mexico to escape his hunters, he stopped at his relatives, the Clements brothers, in Gonzales, Texas. It was early 1871. They suggested he change directions. "They told me I could go to Kansas with cattle and make some money and at the same time be free from arrest," he said. So he took up their offer.

In early March 1871, Hardin and Jim Clements headed for Abilene, Kansas, with 1,200 head of cattle. Jim Clements' brothers Manning, Gip, and Joe followed with another herd. They headed up the Chisholm Trail.

Along the way Hardin recounted his action, telling of gunfights and a manhunt. Hardin told of problems they had in Indian Territory where he left several Indians shot dead. Hardin and his cousins delivered the cattle to North Cottonwood (present Durham), then rode into Abilene for a good time.

There Hardin ran into the more experienced Wild Bill Hickok, age 34, with no serious consequences. In fact, Hardin said they parted as friends. Back at his cattle camp on the North Cottonwood, Hardin heard about a Mexican named Juan Bideno murdering a 22-year-old boss herder named William "Billy" Cohron. So Hardin along with fellow cowboys Jim Rodgers, Hugh Anderson, and Cohron's brother John, decided to hunt down Billy Cohron's killer.

After some detective work, Hardin found out where Bideno was headed. The four avengers rode south heading through Sumner County asking cow herders along the way about the fugitive's whereabouts. Hardin and his friends continued to receive good information from the many trail herders as Hardin pressed on after Bideno.

They stuck close to the Chisholm Trail, which ran slightly west of Wellington. Hardin and the others finally tracked Bideno to Sumner City on the east side of Slate Creek about 10 miles west northwest of Wellington.[4]

After getting information that Bideno was inside the Southwestern Hotel, Hardin entered the dwelling with Hugh Anderson while the others remained outside. Hardin and Anderson first came to the saloon, where Hardin ordered a drink and learned that Bideno was sitting in the restaurant in the back.

"I told my partner to get out his gun and follow me," Hardin said. Recognizing Bideno at a table, Hardin, pistol in hand, called out, "Bideno, I am after you. Surrender." Bideno grabbed for his pistol. Hardin shot him squarely through the forehead.[5]

At that time Joe Thralls, then 23, was in Wellington a few miles southeast, where he and his brother had settled the previous May. East of Kansas, Wyatt Earp was serving his first time as a lawman, having defeated his half brother Newton for the job of constable in Lamar, Missouri in 1870. Bat Masterson, then 17, still lived with his family just northeast of Wichita, Kansas. Bill Tilghman, then also 17, hunted buffalo near Dodge City. At the same time, 13-year-old

Henry Newton Brown, who later rode with Billy the Kid and became a marshal in Caldwell, lived with his relatives near Rolla, Missouri.

Joe Thralls and his brother Elzy then were more concerned about holding on to their quarter section of land east of Wellington than in chasing outlaws. Their first year in Wellington proved to be more of a challenge than they had anticipated. Money and how to make it occupied their time above all else.

While they struggled to survive, they were also aware of the growing outlaw problem in this wide-open prairie around them. There was a noticeable absence of law enforcement. Settlers were more or less on their own. Any character who decided to gain wealth an easier way, whether by stealing horses or cattle and selling them for pure profit, or perhaps by claim jumping for a piece of prime land, found little organized resistance. These growing problems pushed Joe Thralls into his role as a lawman.

Sumner County witnessed this rapidly growing law and order problem between 1871 and 1874. Horse thieves grew from lone wolves to organized bands. Outlaws became increasingly skilled at their job. The Thralls brothers watched this happening. The more they saw of it, the less they liked it. So Joe and his friends did something about it. What they did never became legendary as Wild Bill Hickok, Wyatt Earp, Bat Masterson, or Bill Tilghman. Whether it should have is an open question.

What distinguished Joe from many others was his approach. How he avoided killing or being killed by any of those he hunted down says something about his approach. Scattered throughout old newspapers and accounts by friends are hints of how he did it. Ironically, his very efficiency in tracking down those who strayed from the straight and narrow could be a reason why he never acquired the gunfighter reputation of the more famous lawmen around him.

If longevity were a measure of a leader, Joseph M. Thralls would stand near the front of the line. He was a respected member of his community from his arrival in 1871 till his death nearly 57 years later. That span saw him as a constable, city marshal, deputy sheriff, sheriff, deputy U.S. marshal, a successful cattleman, real estate salesman, and a city mayor. When he died in 1928, a year before Wyatt Earp's death, others would look back on a man held in high esteem throughout most of his life.

If bravery were a measure of a leader, Thralls qualified. He faced danger with seeming equanimity and common sense others often lacked.

If leadership were judged by honesty and consistency toward others, Thralls stood as a prime example. His friends as well as those he chased down attested to that.

Wyatt Earp and Joseph Thralls were different sorts of characters. Thralls stayed in one place, Wellington, for his entire career as a lawman and town leader. He took on duties and responsibilities and stuck to them in good times and bad. He sunk in roots at Wellington. He never worked in a saloon or dance hall. He never gambled.

Earp continued to move throughout his life, from Kansas cow towns (Wichita, Dodge City) to Tombstone, Arizona, Alaska, Colorado, the Dakotas, and California. He had few qualms about making money from bawdy houses, saloons, or gambling, though this took nothing away from his law-keeping abilities.

Wyatt Earp sought publishers for his experiences as a lawman. Shortly before his death, he found someone who wrote down those adventures. And his memory sometimes differed from some of his contemporaries. The man, Stuart Lake, successfully had those adventures published.

Joe Thralls never felt completely comfortable talking about himself. When others interviewed him later in his life, he found it much easier to talk about his friends, such as Bill Hackney, than about himself. So he tended to steer interviewers away from his personal experiences. This made it much harder for anyone to write an exciting account about his more harrowing times.

The people who became friends with Joe Thralls profoundly affected him. Since Thralls had grown up as the oldest offspring in a large family, he took on responsibility for his younger siblings. His friendship with Bill Hackney in Wellington may have provided him with an older sibling model, though this may be getting too psychoanalytical.

One way or another Bill Hackney became one of Thralls' closest friends. Hackney introduced him to the Western way of life. The two men spent a number of days chasing outlaws together.

Thralls had another friend who shared many of his traits. Albert Shenneman served as a fellow law officer who traveled a similar path to becoming sheriff and a similar personality in his job. The two men became close friends, tracking criminals and sharing experiences as neighboring sheriffs for a time.

Besides these friends, Thralls had no trouble finding others throughout his life in Wellington. Those around Thralls had good reason to form a positive view of the lawman. They were drawn to his reserved, steady, consistent personality. They saw an unflinching model of what a peace officer should be.

So Thralls' reserved personality itself weighed in against his becoming a Wild West icon. Wyatt Earp and Bat Masterson could tell stories of their times in saloons, bawdy houses, and gunfights in which people were killed. Masterson could even write about it himself, since he became a newspaper reporter. Both liked to spread stories about their experiences. On the other hand, Joe Thralls never killed anyone, though he came close to it a number of times. And his reserved personality made him hold back on any exuberance or exaggerated stories about his past.

Yet newspaperman Tom A. McNeal, who knew Joe Thralls and interviewed him in the early 1920s, felt Thralls had no peer in his day, no matter how famous the lawman. And Tom McNeal was not alone in this view. He spoke about Thralls toward the end of Thralls' life

"No one would suppose by looking at the rugged form and face of the present mayor of the city of Wellington that he has lived long enough to have been a peace officer and terror to evil doers along the border almost a half century ago," McNeal said. "But the fact is way back in the seventies Joe Thralls had already established a reputation as a hunter of criminals that was known all along the border.

"Cool, tireless, fearless, and yet never reckless, he had a record of generally getting the men he went after, no matter how desperate they were, or how great the difficulties in the way of the man-hunter. In the storehouse of his memory there are many interesting stories."[6]

These stories and the times in which they occurred should be told as a way of restoring a piece of this history. Perhaps this can add a useful layer to the already vast history of America's Old West days.

1

"He said he might spare me $205."

It was November 1868 when 42-year-old Johnson Thralls left his Fairmont, West Virginia home for an uncertain future in the American West. He knew it involved risk. He had a secure life in his West Virginia home.

His parents Isaac and Elizabeth Ann must have taught him to hope and plan for a better life. They evidently valued self-reliance and independence. When his father died in September 1867, Johnson probably already planned to venture west and try his luck. If he hadn't been raised to look for a better life, news from the west could also have pointed him that direction.

Promoters inundated the eastern states with glorious pictures of life out west where almost anyone could afford to start his own farm. Land speculators played their part. It was nearly impossible to avoid the rumors and stories about the advantages of the west. The promoters described Kansas as a land of opportunity. Success stories abounded.

"Homes and wealth awaited everyone in the Shangri La pictured by the railroads!" said historian Ray Allen Billington.[1]

Land grant railroads led the way in boosting frontier Kansas. These railroads stood to profit both from selling land and from creating traffic for their business. So they formed a land department and an immigration bureau to deal with these income sources.

The 1862 Homestead Act allowed each person 160 acres free if they stayed on the land long enough. But often the best land was already occupied by the time many of the settlers needed it. That's where the railroads came in. When settlers couldn't find good open land on which to stake their claim, they could buy it from the railroad usually for $2 to $8 an acre. This was still a lot cheaper than land back East.

The Thralls in West Virginia read about the opportunities out west and heard from people around them about some who had already moved there. All they heard sounded positive.

Johnson Thralls may also have been influenced by his grandfather. Isaac's father, Richard, lived to be 82, dying in July 1835, when Johnson was 10. More than likely Johnson heard stories about his grandfather fighting for United States' independence from England. Richard served in the continental army when George Washington was general.[2] He felt strongly about freedom and the West was the ultimate symbol of that freedom.

Johnson Thralls had few illusions about the hardships that lay ahead when he traveled west. He knew it wouldn't be easy with his wife, Lavinia, and 10 children to take care of. But he also knew that his four oldest children, all boys, were old enough to shoulder some of that responsibility.

According to the 1870 census, the children in 1868 were: Joseph, 20; William E. (nicknamed Elzy), 18; Edward F., 17; Frank W., 15; Mollie, 13; Lewis [Worth T.?], 11; John, 7; Sarah E., 6; and Martha, 2. An 1880 census listed a daughter, Cynthia, who would have also been 6 in 1868.[3]

In November 1868 Johnson left the homestead. His widowed mother Elizabeth went with them. They settled in Paola, Kansas (about 20 miles south of Olathe). Johnson and Lavinia hoped to establish a successful farm and spend the rest of their lives at their new home.

The adventuresome spirit Johnson displayed awakened the same in Joe and Elzy. The boys remained restless even after moving to Paola. They caught a large dose of their father's spirit of adventure.

Their future looked bright. They held it in their own hands. They just had to figure out the details.

Within three years their continuing desire for adventure took on new life. Several Paola businessmen saw southern Kansas as a golden opportunity to prosper. A group of them formed a town company and plotted out an area some 190 miles southwest that would later become Wellington.

After spending time there early in 1871, several returned to Paola and drummed up further interest. They asked for others willing to head west to seek their fortune. It couldn't have come at a better time for Joe and Elzy.

Joe, born on July 11, 1848 (less than four months after Wyatt Earp) and Elzy, born in March 1850 (one year before Morgan Earp), knew they didn't want to stay in Paola. With the scouting party returning with news of wide-open land available, both boys couldn't hide their enthusiasm.

"I was infected with the wanderlust when quite young," Joe later explained. "In the early spring of that year a party of scouts from Paola, headed by C.R. Godfrey and P.A. Wood, came to the new southwest to see if what they had been hearing was true.

"On their return they reported that the half had not been told about the wonderful richness and opportunities of this country – not a settler for miles and miles on the finest land in the world and the pick of any claims on this boundless expanse of rich prairie could be had by going onto it and after one year's settlement pay $1.25 per acre, or $200 for a farm containing 160 acres."[4]

Only part of the Paola party had returned from their southern Kansas journey, but they must have been the best salesmen of the group. "Godfrey and his party stayed long enough on their first trip to locate and lay out Wellington," Joe explained. "When [some] returned to Paola it was for recruits and to move bag and baggage to the new country."

Such talk from these Paola businessmen/salesmen along with the Thralls boys' already overwhelming desire to venture west pushed

Joe and Elzy into action. Their future adventures loomed large in their minds. What they dreamed about would now become reality.

"We were caught by their stories of the short and easy route to a fortune and the desire to get away from the parental nest," Joe explained.[5]

Once the boys showed they were determined to leave, Johnson and Lavinia did all they could to help make their journey a success. "Godfrey was running a drug store in Paola, which was to be transferred to Wellington," said Joe. "That required several teams. My father furnished one team and three settlers."[6]

Scott Cummins, nicknamed the "Pilgrim Bard," also provided several loaded teams. One of them was loaded with barrels of whiskey. Cummins served as the wagon boss and later played a key role in assuring Wellington of winning the county seat.

This Paola group headed west with high hopes. For them, failure was not an option.

Joe remembered the route they took to their destination. " We came via Osawatomie, Garnett, Burlington and Augusta, crossing the Arkansas River . . . northeast of Belle Plaine and across that magnificent valley, where there were yet good claims to be had, to Belle Plaine," he said. "We crossed the Ninnescah . . . west of Belle Plaine, thence southwest to Wellington, crossing the hill six miles north only a short distance east of where the Meridian road now runs and where we could see Slate Creek valley for several miles."[7]

As they neared their destination, the group stopped long enough to contemplate the view from a distance. This would be their permanent home, at least for some. They wanted to remember this moment for the rest of their lives.

"The cavalcade halted for a view of the country we were about to possess." Joe said. "Such a sight it was, there on that bright May day. The dark green, wavy grass, large enough for hay, with two bunches of antelope in sight, made an impression on my mind never to be forgotten."[8]

When Joe arrived at the Wellington site, the only business building standing was Ab and John Shearman's store for traders, the first "mercantile establishment in the infant metropolis." But even it wasn't complete.

"When J.M. Thralls came in about a month [after Shearman started building] the doors and windows were not yet in place, wagon sheets being stretched over the openings to protect the goods and occupants from the weather."[9]

A few weeks after Joe arrived, on June 2nd, Wellington formed a Town Company. This included several from Paola, such as Clark R. Godfrey, P.A. Wood, and R.N. Randall, as well as several who had settled in the area even earlier, including A.A. Jordan, R.A. Davis, and J.P. McCulloch, and L.K. Myers.

Their first year in the area, Joe and Elzy figured the most important goal was to buy some land. They chose a quarter section three miles east of Wellington. Their claim was at the southwest corner of Oxford Road (now highway 160) and Seneca. Officially that was the northeast quarter of section 18 in Avon Township of Sumner County.

They soon learned that claiming land was the easy part. The real struggle had to do with money ($200) to pay for it.

In their struggle, Joe and Elzy not only had to maintain their property. They also had to pay for the land. That meant they had to get a $200 loan, then find some way to pay it back. This provided the biggest challenge to Joe in his first year at Wellington.

For the loan, Joe had to depend on a "friend." With new homesteaders entering southern Kansas in large numbers, it was a sellers' market. Joe soon found out what his friend could do for him.

"We had a friend in Wichita who helped (?) us out, W.C. Woodman," said Thralls. "I went up and laid my case before him. He said he was a little low at that time, having helped so many young men save their claims. I expressed some disappointment at his shortage. Then he said he might spare me $205. When I asked him his interest rate he said 60 per cent. So I borrowed $205 and gave him my note for $328, secured by a mortgage on the 160 acres, due in one year."

15

But that was not the end of Joe's troubles. He couldn't make money fast enough to pay off the loan that first year. So he asked Woodman for an extension.

"At the end of the year [Woodman] would not renew the note," Thralls explained, "but told me one Dyer would make me the loan for a year at 48 per cent. That looked to me as if I would get rich on such cut-rate interest contracts. Of course I had to. I borrowed again."[10]

That first year Joe and Elzy lived in their covered wagon and ate what they could afford, which was very little. They worked at nearly any job others would pay them to do. That included freighting, carpenter work, haying, herding cattle, and working at an implement company.

Sometimes they would park their wagon by a building and sleep inside the building where it was more comfortable. Businessman Horace W. "Harry" Andrews found this out after arriving in town. He came to Wellington on May 19th, 1872. That night he rented an empty shack near Ab W. Shearman's store in town hoping to start his business there. Early next morning, he unexpectedly ran into the Thralls boys.

"Joe Thralls and his brother Elzy had been using it as a sleeping apartment, having their covered wagon parked at the back door," the Wellington paper later explained, "and [they] were a little surprised when Harry came in that morning and routed them out, informing them that he was in possession, and they had to take the rest of their beauty sleep on in the wagon."[11]

Since odd jobs along with their struggle to hold on to their claim filled the Thralls boys' days, they had little time for anything else. But Joe couldn't help but notice a growing lawlessness around him. Most often this took the form of roving bands of horse thieves.

In September 1871 two horses and a mule were stolen in the middle of town. The bold thieves fled to Shoo Fly Creek and on into Indian Territory to the south. This became a favorite escape route. Many in town suspected an organized band of thieves was behind this and other thefts that became increasingly common.[12]

"He said he might spare me $205."

"Horse thieves are becoming quite bold east of us," the Oxford paper editorialized. Homesteaders began to feel increasing desperation toward this common crime.[13]

2

Hackney sets an example

Joe Thralls couldn't stand by while outlaws ran over the homesteaders around Wellington. Sometime during his second year in town he became a constable. The *Oxford Times* in September listed him serving along with D. [Daniel William] Jones. Other county and town leaders included William P. Hackney, county representative; Reuben Riggs, county attorney; Ab W. Shearman, town trustee; and Vann Smith, justice of the peace.[1]

Though G.A. Hamilton held the official title of Sumner County Sheriff, in reality he had quit serving before his term expired. In the vacuum, Andrew A. Jordan took up the position and town leaders recognized him as sheriff. That's why the paper called him that.

Usually constables in the township county seat doubled as deputy sheriffs. Thralls and Jones were no exception. Both helped out Jordan whenever he needed a posse to track down lawbreakers. Often the ranking constable would become city marshal. By the following year, 1873, Dan Jones became Wellington city marshal.

Joe Thralls learned much of his law enforcement ability from both acting Sheriff Jordan and fellow lawman Dan Jones. Both developed reputations as lawmen.

Andrew A. Jordan was a Civil War veteran who lost an arm fighting for the Confederate Army. He drifted north and settled on a quarter section later on the west side of Wellington before it became a town. He was one of the eight men who formed the Wellington Town Company. The others were Dr. P.A. Wood, Captain L.K.

19

Myers, Dr. Clark R. Godfrey, Major A.N. Randall, John S. McMahan, and John P. McCulloch.

Jordan was the third Sumner County sheriff. J.J. Ferguson held the position from September 26, 1871 till November 7, when George A. Hamilton became the first elected sheriff. Hamilton appointed Jordan an under-sheriff, but then resigned on April 11, 1872. Jordan took over till John G. Davis, from Oxford, was elected November 4, 1872.[2]

Jordan, according to the local paper, "made quite a record as a fearless upholder of the majesty of the law. He used to go around with two heavy navy revolvers strapped to his belt and as he was known to be a dead shot in spite of his crippled right arm, lawbreakers made it convenient to give him a wide berth."[3] He was later described as "the most fearless and best officer in the history of the county."[4]

Joe Thralls' fellow constable Dan Jones was a couple years older than Joe. Evidently Jones held the higher position. Within a year he became the Wellington city marshal. By the middle 1870s he moved south to Red Fork Ranch in Indian Territory but moved again north to Caldwell, Kansas in 1880. According to those who knew him, he continued to serve as a lawman, being a deputy U.S. marshal. In Caldwell he again became a constable and seemed to attract trouble, being accused of more than one killing.

◊

Though these fellow lawmen gave Thralls valuable lessons in his job, another man who was not a lawman perhaps taught him more than both Jordan and Jones. During Joe Thralls first few years as a constable, William Patrick "Bill" Hackney rode with him in posses on more than one occasion though Hackney never pinned on a badge.

Hackney worked as a lawyer but it didn't prevent him from joining posses to chase outlaws. He had first-hand experience with the lawlessness out west before Joe Thralls arrived in Wellington.

When he later became friends with Thralls, he shared his experiences. His views and his attitude toward challenges colored Thralls views.

Bill Hackney, born in Iowa in 1842, was six years older than Joe Thralls. In 1850 he moved to Illinois with his father. In 1861 he joined the army as a private and four years later left as captain. While fighting in the Civil War for the Union those four years he was twice injured in battles.

He fought in the battles of Fort Henry, Fort Donelson, Shiloh, Corinth, Nashville, Altoona Pass, Wise's Forks and others. At Altoona Pass on October 5th, 1864, one ball went through his right cheek and one through his body.[5]

Between 1865 and 1870 he learned to be a lawyer. He then decided to leave Illinois for the west.

He journeyed to Kansas in 1870. "I arrived in Emporia on the first passenger train running over the Santa Fe from Topeka there, thence to Eureka by stage, next to El Dorado and then to Winfield," he said. "There were only seven shacks in the town, big and little, hence I went on to Arkansas City, where I stayed all night expecting to return next morning."[6]

But Hackney's feisty outlook took over that morning. He was one who never liked to be pushed around though he was a small man.

During breakfast he met a man named Lafe Goodrich. As soon as Goodrich found out Hackney was a lawyer he hired him. Goodrich had recently laid claim to the northwest quarter section of the Arkansas City town site. Now he needed to defend that claim. The Claim League, made up of claim holders in town who were trying to protect their land from claim jumpers, summoned Goodrich to appear before them. Goodrich hoped Hackney was a good lawyer.

When the local homesteaders found out Hackney, a new man in town, was defending Goodrich, they were furious. They wanted to deal with Hackney the way they dealt with horse thieves.

21

"Every one was up in arms against me and they declared he [Goodrich] ought to be hung and I ought to be hanged with him," said Hackney. "I was in for it and I faced the music that night probably before five hundred men, and it ended in a big row in which I was the central figure."

Hackney didn't look like much of a challenge to the up-in-arms homesteaders. The 28-year-old Illinoisan weighed less than 130 pounds wet. But the town soon found out what kind of man Hackney was. As a war veteran and adventurer, he had never backed down from a challenge and he wasn't about to start. What he said or did is not recorded, but he survived that first night.

"With my usual luck, [I] escaped unhurt," is all Hackney said.[7]

The next morning Hackney had planned to leave by stage for Winfield where he wanted to homestead. But when town leaders threatened him, he changed his plans. A committee composed of several people, including the postmaster and the stage line manager, came up to him that morning and told him to leave town as quickly as he could if he valued his life. That was the wrong thing to say to Hackney.

Without hesitation, Hackney told them he already planned to leave that morning for Winfield. But since they threatened him, he would stay in Arkansas City until everyone got acquainted with him.

"Within two hours I had selected lots without consulting anybody, hired a man to make the foundation and a carpenter to build me a house," he said. "And that day [I] sent to Illinois for my wife and her mother, and I stayed [in Arkansas City] until they got acquainted with me."[8]

Bill Hackney soon became involved in politics. "I was a delegate to the first Republican convention in that county which met at Dexter to elect two delegates to a state convention where they nominated state officers and members of congress," he said, "and I was secretary of the second Republican convention in that county that met to nominate county officers."[9]

But his political involvement was soon overshadowed by his involvement with vigilantes. In December 1870 several vigilantes accused of killing suspected horse thieves around Douglass, Kansas, hired Hackney to defend them. The vigilantes' actions dated back to early November.[10]

The small town of Douglass looked inviting to outlaws, especially horse thieves. The town stood several miles southeast of Wichita. The thinly populated area around it with a number of waterways running through it, including the Walnut River, seemed to welcome outlaws.

Organized bands of horse thieves could hide out easily and move stolen livestock with little chance of being caught. Homesteaders in the area became increasingly frustrated. When their livestock disappeared, they couldn't seem to do anything about it. By 1870 these horse thieves seemed to have more power than the law.

One day late in 1870 settlers decided enough was enough. They banded together, calling themselves the "Regulators." They watched for clues as to who was behind the stolen horses. The "Regulators" took a no nonsense approach. They had come out of the Civil War with experience in tracking down thieves. .

The law in the area was supposed to deal with this crime. But few had any faith in it. The local law, made up of Butler County Sheriff James Thomas, 35, and town constable Peter W. Harpool, seemed unable to meet the challenge.

Some of the questionable characters roaming around the Douglass area in 1870 included brothers Lewis and George Booth, fellow traveler Jack "California Joe" Corbin, and James Smith. James Mead, one of the early settlers in Wichita, said he knew Smith as a "desperado." Mead later described him as a man who "never did anything else but steal, gamble, and murder since he was a boy." The *Wichita Vidette* (November 10, 1870) said "Smith and Corbin were around here for several days previous and left here about noon of Tuesday (November 8, 1870), Smith riding off a horse (that was) 'U.S. property' ... which he had borrowed from one Wallingford."

As more livestock turned up missing in November 1870, the "Regulators" geared up for action. They had local citizens behind them. One event then gave them the incentive to act.

Early in November several men stole mules from P.W. Crawford and his two sons, William D. and James F., while they were in Wichita. Crawford later found the mules in town and took them back. Shortly after that James Smith, Jack Corbin, George Corbin, and one other man caught up with Crawford, knocked him off his horse with a revolver, and threatened to kill him if he didn't give them his horse and those that Crawford's sons were riding.

The two sons galloped away with the outlaws chasing them. The sons reached their camp before the outlaws caught up. The Crawfords drove off the outlaws and rescued their father.

That was not all. The next night thieves stole all three teams from the Crawfords.

Tuesday, November 8, was Election Day. People in Douglass voted at the Douglass House Hotel. That afternoon P.W. Crawford happened to be in town and told his story about the horse thieves. While he talked, Jack Corbin entered the room, walked past the group listening to Crawford, then walked out the door.

"That's one of the thieves that stole from me," Crawford told the others. In the group listening were some of the "Regulators."

That evening after the Booth brothers and Corbin rode out of town going four miles north to the Booth homestead, others in town followed. Another group of townspeople went two miles east to the James Smith homestead. When they found no one at home, they retraced their path back to Slayton's Crossing where they figured Smith would eventually pass on his way home. They hid and waited.

The vigilantes who headed towards the Booth homestead waited till about 9 p.m. when the Booths would be in bed. Then they walked up to the house and knocked on the door. Lewis Booth's wife Jane answered. Her daughters Jesse, three, and Mary, one, were also asleep inside. The vigilantes pushed Jane aside and asked the Booths and Corbin to surrender. They did.

The "Regulators" marched the three men toward the Walnut River some 200 yards away. They put a rope around Corbin's neck and looped it over a sycamore limb. They lifted him, dropped him, then kept him from choking and asked for names of other horse thieves. They repeated this several times. When the "Regulators" figured they'd pumped him dry, they let him hang.

The Booth brothers watched. As Corbin dangled in the wind, the Booths begged to be shot. When it looked like the Regulators were about to oblige, the Booths suddenly bolted for cover. The vigilantes filled them with bullets.

Back at Slayton's Crossing the other vigilantes heard hoof beats from the south. One in the group watched from a closer position as the rider approached. He was to identify the rider before shooting. If he shot, the rest would follow.

Just as the rider entered the water, the front man shot. Smith staggered in the saddle, drew his pistol, and shot toward the flash of light. The rest of the group pumped Smith full of lead. Smith fell by the river dead. One of the vigilantes pinned a note on his shirt. It read, "Shot for a horse thief."

An inquest held the next day concluded the four men came to their deaths at the hands of unknown persons. Most neighbors agreed with the vigilante action, but not all.

Some in Douglass saw the vigilantes as murderers. Among the critics were William G. Quimby, Mike Drea, Dr. James T. Morris, and Morris's son, Alexander. Quimby decided to do something about it.

Quimby, an early settler in the Douglass area, owned a general merchandise store in the middle of town. Mike Drea was a clerk in the store. Alexander Morris owned a drugstore across the street from Quimby. Dr. Morris helped his son get started in the business. They weren't the only ones who believed the vigilantes were murderers, but they were the most vocal.

Three of the four men killed November 8 owed Quimby more than $800. Quimby hired a lawyer to help him collect. He and his lawyer made trips out of town in the process.

Quimby's travels and his views about the vigilantes made others take notice. Rumors spread that Quimby and others were part of the horse thief ring. Dr. James Morris, who had treated a wounded "Regulator," became a suspect when he rode throughout the area speaking out against vigilante justice.

Quimby's lawyer got warrants for the arrest of 87 men and one woman. Among those 87 was the stage driver who was passing by as the vigilantes were crossing the Walnut River. The stage driver hired Hackney to defend him.

Hackney and the stage driver headed to Douglass along with bondsmen H.B. Norton and a Dr. Leonard. Hackney was ready to defend the stage driver but he never got the chance.

"When we got [to Douglass] the case was postponed for ten days," said Hackney. The stage driver and bondsmen returned to Arkansas City and Hackney stayed at the Lambo Hotel in Douglass at the request of other vigilantes. These vigilantes hired Hackney to draw up warrants for Quimby, Dray, Morris, and his son, charging them with horse theft.

Hackney went to a hearing before Justice of the Peace J.L. Johnson about the warrants Hackney issued. It ended in a 15-day continuance. Each side threatened the other.

Thursday, December 1, 1870, the fight between these factions became deadly. The weather had been mild for that time of year. That day, though, Hackney noticed an approaching storm. He went for a walk on the northwest side of town. When he returned, some vigilantes blocked his way. Years later Hackney remembered the whole incident.

"As I came back, Burney Dunn and two others in advance of a big crowd met me and Burney said: 'We want you to get out of this town at once and don't stand on the order of your going.' At that time to accuse a man of being interested in horse thieves was equivalent almost to anything. First thought that occurred to my mind was somebody had made a report against me and I said to him: 'I have not gone on the order of any human being since my father used to tell me to go, excepting when I was in the war and subject to superiors' orders. I came there on legitimate business and have done nothing to justify my leaving the county, and I'll be damned if I'll go away before I'm ready.'

"He [Burney Dunn] then said, 'Hackney, don't be a damn fool; we have heretofore spoken to you about defending us and for reasons satisfactory to ourselves we don't want you here,' and he pulled out $150 in gold, the first I had seen for many years, and said, 'Take this and select any horse you want and it is yours.' There was a very fine big road horse with new saddle and blanket near by and I said, 'I will take that roan horse.' He said, 'It's yours,' and I replied, 'What does the owner say?' to which he answered, 'I am the owner and it is yours.' I then said, "A storm is coming and I have no overcoat,' and he said to a fellow about my size, 'Jim, get out of that overcoat and let him have it.' He did so, and then I said, 'I have no gun,' and another fellow unstrapped a very fine pair of ivory handled revolvers and gave them to me. Another fellow took off his spurs and fastened them on my feet, and I then told them I needed some gloves. I was furnished with a fine pair, and I said, 'What about my hotel bill?' They replied, 'That will be paid.'

"I remembered Mark Twain who described the vigilance committee in Nevada when they left one fellow go and hanged the rest. They brought his horse, food and a revolver, and told him to get on that horse and they would give him 15 minutes to get away and if they ever caught him back there again they would kill him. He vaulted into his saddle, lifted his hat and said, 'Gentlemen, if this damn bronco don't buck, five minutes is all I need." I vaulted into my saddle, lifted my hat and replied, 'If this damn horse don't buck I will be gone mighty quick,' and away I went."[11]

After Hackney left, the "Regulators" captured the four men and held them in Quimby's store. That night about 200 of the vigilantes took the four from the store and headed south.

About a mile and a half away near Joshua Olmstead's sawmill they stopped. Some in the mob laid a board from the sawmill between the limbs of two trees, which stood close together. They looped four ropes over it. About 2 a.m. Friday they lynched the four men.

Wichita leading citizen James Mead agreed with the vigilantes. He sent a letter to Kansas Governor James Harvey.

"Do not give yourself too much uneasiness as to the doings of the vigilance committee on lower Walnut in Butler Co.," he wrote. "They are doing good service in ridding the country of a set of organized Horse Thieves, murderers and desperadoes of at least six years standing to my knowledge."

He concluded that the action of the "Regulators" in Walnut Valley "is simply the vengeance of an outraged and plundered community, who finding the Law a mere farce, have executed summary Justice on a set of villains who make robbing their business and who do not hesitate to kill innocent men who seek to bring them to justice."

The Douglass killings received statewide attention. People from northern and eastern Kansas expressed concern over what they conceived as "lawlessness" in southern Kansas.

Hackney partly agreed. On December 16, the *Emporia News* ran an article from Arkansas City dated December 9. Titled "The Late Trouble in Butler County" and signed by "W.P.," its content indicated Bill Hackney as author.

Hackney defended Arkansas City as a desirable place to live. He contrasted it with what happened in Douglass. Speaking of Arkansas City, he said, "A kinder, more hospitable, or on the whole, better class of people, I have nowhere found in Kansas."

In contrast, he added, "But on the western frontier of Kansas, extending as it is said from Junction City into the Indian Territory, there is an organization of thieves, constituting the greatest of all draw-backs to the peace and prosperity of this, otherwise, most prominent region. For years the desperate reign of these desperadoes has been undisturbed. Seldom has the law even so much as arrested them, and never, it is said, placed the first one in the place appointed for thieves and robbers."[12]

He then fingered several in Douglass as part of that ring of thieves. "Two of them four or five weeks ago, at Emporia, stole the last dime ($65) a poor teamster had, and at the trial for the crime, were promptly turned loose to resume the practice of their profession," he said. "The next thing I heard as they returned to Wichita and Douglass was of the detection of four of the gang, two Booths, Corbin, and Smith.

"In two or three weeks after this a number of honest citizens were arrested, charged by one of the thieves (as is generally believed) with murdering his four comrades. About the same time one Quimby, a leading merchant in Douglass, Mike Dray, his partner, Dr. Morris and his son, were arrested, tried, and held to bail for stealing horses. While being guarded that they might procure bail, Quimby and his wife made strong threats of raising their clan and taking vengeance upon the citizens, who were staking their all on 'cleaning out' the thieves.

"On Thursday night [December 2] some 70 men came to relieve the guard, and end the practices of these wretched men. The [men] were hung a mile and a half south of Douglass. This makes eight of the band that have been put out of the way lately, and I am assured by the best of citizens, that the battle being joined, never will they [citizens] hold up, nor cry enough till it is decided whether thieves or honest men are to rule the valley, and upon this frontier."[13]

Hackney added a detail about one of the accused thieves that must have come from vigilantes at the lynching. "Corbin confessed and gave the names of some 50 of his clan, told where would be found stolen stock, and so it was," said Hackney, "Hence it would seem, since they have deliberately and persistently outlawed all order and law, they have no right to complain that honest citizens deal to them summary justice, though not in accordance with the forms of law."[14]

Hackney's views on horse thieves and vigilante justice couldn't help but rub off on Joe Thralls when they got to know each other shortly after that.

29

Hackney's chief concern that November 1870, though, was with politics and his position among his peers. The election results told him Arkansas City would never be the county seat. He decided to go to a place that looked more promising.

"I decided to go into Sumner County to help organize that and locate a town for the county seat, the census of 1870 showing only twenty-one people in the county," he said.

He along with three friends, J. L. (Jim) and George Alexander Hamilton, and a Mr. Lambertson, left Arkansas City on the first day of the year, 1871. They headed west hoping to find a place with more promise. Lambertson drove a covered wagon pulled by a team of horses while Bill Hackney and his friends rode horseback.

The trip was a struggle from the beginning. The ground had recently frozen and was now thawing out. They had to trudge through this muck as they headed west. They kept moving till they reached near the future site of South Haven. The cold wind forced them to camp on the grounds of a dry creek for shelter.

Next morning they traveled to the Chikaskia River, then continued along it till they reached the Barrington Ranch on the Chisholm Trail. There they stopped for dinner. After eating, they followed the Chisholm Trail to Slate Creek, crossed it where Sumner City was located, and continued to a cow ranch about a mile away. They spent the night there.

In the morning they went northeast to what was then Prairie Creek (which emptied into the Ninnescah) and stopped for dinner. Then they continued on to Cook's Grove, crossed the river, and went to what would become the town site of Belle Plaine.

Bill Hackney and the others thought this would be a good place to locate the county seat. Lambertson claimed to be a surveyor. He measured the area. (Hackney later learned Lambertson miscalculated. They weren't as close to the center of the county as they thought).

The four men then worked out a plot for the town. They chose 17 quarter sections for future settlers as well as a half section in the middle for the town site. Because Lambertson had provided the wagon and team, the others let him choose first. He took land next to the south quarter of the town site. Hackney chose the quarter section south of Lambertson's for himself and one east for his mother-in-law.

When all were finished choosing, Lambertson stayed at the site. The others returned to Arkansas City to settle up and move their families.

While these early activities of Hackney and his friends established the beginning of what would become Belle Plaine, it didn't become official till March 1871. According to Cutler's *History*, that's when the Belle Plaine Town Company started. Besides Hackney, James L. Hamilton, and George Alexander Hamilton, it included J.C. Thurman, J.M. Lewis, W.E. Chamberlin, J.L. Kellogg, and E.M. Miller[15]

Bill Hackney traded his Arkansas City home for a pony, two cattle, and a wagon. He bought as much lumber as he could afford for his house. He hired another man to haul lumber for his mother-in-law's place.

Hackney had a surprise waiting for him when he arrived back at the Belle Plaine town site. A big Texan had jumped Hackney's mother-in-law's place. Hackney reacted the way he always did.

He berated the Texan as only he could, using articulate, well-placed curses, lambasting him from head to toe. The two then started throwing punches. But Hackney was no match for the king-size Texan.

"It did not take long for him to do me up," said Hackney, "but as soon as I got my breath I went at him again with the same result, and a third time I tackled him with a like result. In the meantime my eyes were swelling so I could hardly see, my left ankle and right wrist were out of business. I could see some guns leaning against a tree, so I made for the guns and he made for the timber. It turned out the boys had pulled the shots out of the guns. I would have shot him if I could. I then announced when I came back ready for business that if he was on that claim I would kill him."[16]

31

By the fall of 1871 people in Sumner as well as Cowley County knew about Bill Hackney. He made friends with most people he met and developed a reputation of being an outstanding lawyer, not just because he was the first one in Belle Plaine. He soon tried to do something about his political ambitions.

In November he ran for state representative and won. In that position he became friends with city, county, and state officials. That included lawmen, whether city marshals, township constables, or county sheriff.

Hackney's first year as state representative coincided with Joe Thralls' first year as a lawman. Though Hackney lived in Belle Plaine, as state representative he regularly traveled to Wellington, the temporary county seat till citizens chose it in April 1872. Joe Thralls and Bill Hackney soon became life long friends.

3

"The execution had a salutary effect."

Rapid changes marked the early 1870s in Sumner County, Kansas. Settlers staked their claims, keeping a watchful eye on surrounding dangers. Citizens decided who would be their leaders. Thousands of cowboys trailed cattle through the county from Texas to Abilene. Land speculators had a field day.

With all this going on, one of the greatest threats to order was the growing presence of horse thieves. The migrations and recent settlements in southern Kansas provided an ideal opportunity for such predators. Homesteaders provided the perfect prey.

Settlers struggled to make a life for themselves. They not only faced life-threatening diseases and financial hardships. While trying to make a living, they also had to look over their shoulders for hostile Indians as well as ambitious outlaws.

Many of the settlers lived in dugouts by creeks or sod houses on the prairie. Few had the resources to construct wood buildings for themselves. Wellington itself had few permanent buildings. That meant settlers had to stake hitch their horses under a roughly built lean-to or out in the open. This left horse thieves with abundant opportunities to ply their trade. The only defense left to settlers seemed to be a strong offense – vigilante justice dealt swiftly, surely, and unequivocally whenever a thief could be caught in the act.

Threats from hostile Indians remained an ever-present reality. These Indians saw the settlers as invaders who endangered their way of life. The Indians did what they could to prevent further intrusion on their land by trying to discourage others from living there.

Two Osage Indians tried to kill a man named "Dutch" Fred Crats living on Bluff Creek near Caldwell in June 1871. Fred owned a ranch where he sold liquor to the Indians. Trouble between him and this tribe led to this attack, according to witnesses. The Indians managed to shoot Crats in the back and send an arrow through one arm and shoulder. Crats survived though he was permanently disabled.[1]

In July, Sumner City, near Wellington and on the Chisholm Trail, saw plenty of violence. That's where John Wesley Hardin shot Juan Bideno. Also someone shot and killed a cowboy suspected of stealing a horse.[2] In August, a claim jumper near Wellington shot the owner when the owner tried to repossess his land.[3]

In September, two horses and a mule were stolen in the middle of Wellington. While no violence occurred, this act in the center of town spoke volumes to the homesteaders. Most were convinced that organized bands of horse thieves were behind it. These incidents continued to increase rapidly. The thieves usually fled south to Shoo Fly Creek near the border and disappeared.[4]

In November in Sumner City, L.C. Hopkins shot and severely wounded Jake Starlight. They had argued about who owned a horse. Witnesses testified Hopkins was justified, so he was never arrested.[5]

Years later, Joe Thralls told Tom A. McNeal, author of *When Kansas Was Young*, about the first recorded murder in Wellington. It happened in May 1872. The details Thralls used indicated he had firsthand knowledge. By that time Thralls, along with Dan William Jones, was a township constable responsible for helping keep order in the Wellington area.

According to Thralls, one Friday two hunters came to Wellington ready for action. One named Smith, the other nicknamed

"Red Shirt" Blanchard, were looking for action. That day they ran into a notorious gambler named Lynch. The men drank and gambled together and eventually began to quarrel.

Lynch himself was no soft touch. Thralls described him as "a gambler and all-round tough who owned a race horse and went swaggering around with a pair of revolvers belted on as part of his dress."[6]

After gambling and drinking all day and into the evening, around 9 p.m. Smith and Lynch both drew their guns in the saloon. Someone (possibly Thralls or Jones) stopped them from shooting each other. Both men swore to finish the job later.

Gun in hand, Lynch went out the north front door of the saloon, turned east, walked a few feet, then stood in a shadow watching the door. A few minutes later Smith walked to the door. In a flash, Lynch fired. He was 10 feet away. The ball went through the pine door and hit Smith in the chest.

Lynch figured he'd killed Smith and ran northwest across the public square. His gun went off two more times. Thralls figured that was accidental since the bullets went through both of Lynch's feet.

Meantime, in the saloon Smith yelled, "I'm shot" before he discovered the bullet went through his outside clothes and stopped at his undershirt. Realizing he was unhurt, he pulled his gun and ran south out the saloon's back door in search of Lynch. He spotted a man to the east, shot and killed him instantly. The man happened to be named Maxwell, not Lynch. Maxwell lived on the Chikaskia River and came to town to raise money for his neighbors who had lost their belongings in a prairie fire.

Now Smith was in a pinch. Being the kind of person he was, he knew what to do. He and his friend "Red Shirt" told the gathering crowd their story. Lynch, they said, just shot and killed the poor man Maxwell and deserved to die. The crowd bought the story.

Lawmen, including Joe Thralls, took Lynch into custody as much for Lynch's safety as for his "crime." Knowing what might happen next, the lawmen spirited Lynch away for safekeeping.

The crowd dispersed that night. Next day, townspeople began to congregate. Smith and Blanchard knew what to do. They rode out of town.

Some in town knew the two hunters were mixed up in the killing and thought they should take some of the blame. These townsmen formed a posse and rode after them. The posse followed Smith and Blanchard for 20 to 30 miles before the trail went cold. The posse returned ready to do business with Lynch.

By midnight Saturday more than a hundred vigilantes talked about their next move. They were determined to get Lynch.

Sunday morning the mob found where Lynch was being held. They took him by force. Lynch knew his time was up. He asked for a lawyer to make out his will. The vigilantes agreed.

The first lawyer Lynch asked for, D. Newton Caldwell, refused the job. He claimed he was too inexperienced. A few years later he would become the Sumner County Attorney. Judge Reuben Riggs, then serving as County Attorney, agreed to help. Lynch left everything to his sister.

The mob then put Lynch on his horse. With two rows of guards on both sides of the condemned man, the mob led him to some trees by Slate Creek. They put a rope around his neck, fastened the other end to a limb, and shooed away the horse. In this case, newspaper headlines could have read "Lynch Lynched."

Joe Thralls had mixed feelings about the event. "Although the real murderer was not hanged, the execution had a salutary effect on evil doers for years afterward," he said. "Still it can hardly be said that justice had been satisfied, for the man who did murder Maxwell still lives."[7]

◊

In 1873 Thralls was serving as a constable when a cowboy near Wellington was murdered. Lawman Thralls would continue to pursue the killer for the next seven years. It would bring out one of his strongest traits, persistence in the face of a seemingly hopeless

situation. At this time Constable Thralls also served on Sheriff John
G. Davis' posses and helped the sheriff whenever called on assist
him in catching criminals. Thralls fellow constable Dan W.
Jones by 1873 served as Wellington's city marshal.

In the summer of that year (1873) Hezekiah G. Williams and
James J. Elkins had 2,000 head of Texas cattle at Williams' ranch
10 miles southwest of Wellington. One of the cowboys watching
the cattle was a Wellington man named William McDowell. His
wife, Maria C. McDowell, worked as a cook for the cattle camp.

Saturday morning, July 19, 1873 Maria was working alone at the
ranch. Only the owner, Hezekiah Williams, was home. That day
Williams tried to take advantage of Maria. She defended herself as
best she could and told Williams in no uncertain terms she was
going to tell her husband. Williams threatened her.

"You know, it wouldn't cost much to hire another herder to kill
your husband," he said. But she refused to let Williams frighten
her. As soon as she had the chance she told her husband.

Next morning, Sunday, July 20th, the cattleman Williams left his
ranch never to return. That night Williams' partner James Elkins
sent William McDowell on an errand with another hired hand,
Texas cowboy Willis Jackson, telling them to get supplies. Jackson
returned about midnight, alone.

Monday morning, July 21st, Elkins gave Jackson "the best horse
in the outfit" for him to head south on the Chisholm Trail along with
other cowboys returning to Texas. After riding along with them till
noontime, Elkins said goodbye, turned around, and headed to
Wichita.

Maria McDowell returned to her home in Wellington later that
day. She became worried when William hadn't come home by
evening. She didn't wait long before reporting him missing. She
already suspected foul play. For a woman out west in the 19th
century she showed amazing courage.

No doubt she felt desperate. She had two children to raise,
Harper and Lillie May. Now she had a missing husband and

suspected her threats against her molester had something to do with it.

On Tuesday, July 22nd, Maria filed charges against Hezekiah Williams. She stated that Williams "did unlawfully, willfully, and feloniously and with force and arms assault plaintiff and did then and there willfully, unlawfully, and feloniously and against the will and consent of plaintiff forcibly ravish and carnally know plaintiff to her damage in the sum of ten thousand dollars."[8] She filed a $10,000 suit against Williams for damages.

Wellington citizens formed a search party and began looking for the missing man. They kept up the search till Thursday, July 24th. That day they found William McDowell one and a half miles north of Williams' ranch. He lay dead with a bullet hole in the back of his head. The last man known to have been with McDowell was Willis Jackson.

That same day, July 24th, Maria went to court and filed another lawsuit and the court issued a summons for the arrest of Williams, Elkins, and Willis Jackson for damages resulting from their murder of her husband. In the suit Maria included as plaintiffs herself, her two children, and "next friend" George McDowell. The purpose of the suit was to recover damages "for injuries arising from the commission of a felony viz the felonious killing of the said William McDowell" from the defendants who were now "residents of the state of Texas."

In her complaint, Maria went into more detail. The suit said the defendants "did on the 19th and 20th days of July, 1873, conspire and confederate together at the county of Sumner aforesaid for the express purpose of feloniously taking the life of the said William McDowell... That in pursuance of said conspiracy and to carry out said design and agreement they ... compelled the said William McDowell to leave his home and proceed to the town of Austin in said county of Sumner and that afterwards to wit on the 20th day July, 1873, ... defendant James J. Elkins assaulted the said William McDowell with ... a large revolver and did then and there feloniously beat, bruise, and wound the said William McDowell...

And that afterwards ... with the aid, counsel, and assistance of defendants James J. Elkins and Hezekiah G. Williams, defendant Willis Jackson did feloniously assault ... William McDowell with a ... loaded revolver ... did shoot, kill, and murder ... William McDowell to the damage of these plaintiffs in the sum of ten thousand dollars.

"Plaintiffs therefore ask judgment for the sum of ten thousand dollars and for their costs and that an order of attachment issue against the property of defendants."[9]

Under-Sheriff William H. McClelland, summons in hand, and probably with the help of Joe Thralls, Andrew Jordan, and other lawmen, searched for Williams, Elkins, and Jackson for a week. On August 2nd, 1873, McClelland returned the summons, stating that "I have made diligent search and the within named can not be found in my county."

Two days later, July 26th, at 8 a.m., Sheriff John Davis along with Andrew A. Jordan and John A. Kirk, enacted the order of attachment. They went to Williams' ranch where they possessed and appraised the personal property. Sheriff Davis listed the following:

1,850 head of Texas cattle from two to six years old road branded W & E appraised at $12.50 each, $23, 125.

1 yoke work cattle, $40.

31 head of ponies at $20 each, $620.

1 ox wagon with camp equipment, $50.

2 saddles at $5 each, $10.

Total value, $23,845.

By this time Thralls had learned a few things from Sheriff Davis, Andrew Jordan, and very likely from Dan Jones and Bill Hackney as well. Thralls knew the lawmen around him had tried to find Willis Jackson and the others as best they could. Yet Thralls had to feel frustrated by the fact that none of the lawmen could catch the culprits.

This played on his mind. It made him more determined than ever to get to the bottom of this crime. He made note of the incident as unfinished business to be resolved in the future. This determination marked his character throughout his career as a lawman.

Thralls knew the danger of following someone south through Indian Territory and on to Texas. He heard his friends talk about rampant lawlessness in Indian Territory where the worst of the lot hid out. This was a couple of years before Judge Isaac Parker sent deputies into the area in an attempt to tame it down. Travellers through this area risked more than robbery. Joe knew about roaming Indians as well as white outlaws who sought refuge from the law in this Territory.

Though Joe was willing to track Jackson then and there, he didn't have enough information to go on. Besides, he was a township constable, not a sheriff. He had no authority to track criminals beyond his township.

From that time till the conclusion of his quest for Jackson, Thralls showed dogged determination. He displayed signs of a modern day detective in digging up every scrap of information he could find about Jackson's background and travels. He following leads from other lawmen and other Jackson acquaintances. He saved those scraps as he continued his search for Jackson.

◊

The surrounding danger in Kansas was bad enough to scare off some good men. Rumour had spread that the first Sumner county sheriffs, including Ferguson and Hamilton, had cut short their service out of fear for their lives.

All along the Chisholm Trail and surrounding area cowboys rode herd and outlaws plied their trade. Some of those given to crime stole horses and cattle. Others held up stagecoaches. Still others used intimidation to jump land claims. Whatever the form of crime, lawmen had their hands full. Violence became an integral part of life where law was absent or poorly organized.

"The execution had a salutary effect."

Shooting incidents often got little attention. For example, on August 16, 1873 a Mexican shot and killed a Texas cattle herder named Reddis at Oges Camp on the Ninnescah River. The Mexican rode off. A couple of days later Ike Walker, a frontiersman who was accustomed to violence, saw the Mexican with another friend on Slate Creek just south of Wellington. Walker knew about Reddis' death and the killer's identity. Walker recognized the man and killed both him and his friend.[10]

So those first years as a lawman (1872 and 1873) challenged young Joe Thralls to develop his character and techniques. Citizens recognized Thralls' skills and increasingly supported him. But his greatest challenges lay ahead of him.

4

"Bill's language almost made us shudder."

People in southern Kansas panicked in 1874. Like the Philistines after David killed Goliath, they fled for their lives. They had just received news that Indians were on the warpath and heading their direction.

Trouble had been brewing for the last several months before clear signs of violence showed up. The present problems rose from several causes. An incident at Adobe Walls in the staked plains of the Texas panhandle provided an example.

By 1874 Indians on the southern plains, including Kansas, northern Indian Territory (Oklahoma), and the Texas panhandle, were becoming increasingly restless. They had several good reasons.

Repeatedly land the U.S. government promised to Indians had white settlers on it. Buffalo hunters around Dodge City continued to follow the thinning buffalo herds even when this led to off-limits land. Meanwhile horse thieves from southern Kansas increasingly stole horses from Indians. Add to all that unscrupulous traders who brought whiskey, guns, and ammunition to the plains Indians for a price, and it made for a bad brew.

When Dodge City merchants decided to invest in a venture to the southwest, they knew they were taking a risk. The U.S. government promised not to enter the Texas panhandle where Cheyenne and other tribes hunted the diminishing buffalo herds. By spring 1874 the merchants and buffalo hunters looked south for more business.

Among the buffalo hunters traveling southwest was Billy Dixon. Dixon had been on edge ever since word spread that Indians would challenge any buffalo hunters who went after the southern herds. But that didn't stop him. Dixon was young (23), daring, and wasn't about to quit doing what had brought him a successful living. So off he went.

As he and other hunters moved south, businessmen in Dodge City took the opportunity. It was early March 1874 when Dodge City merchants A.C. "Charlie" Myers along with Jim Hanrahan, Tom O'Keefe, and 50 buffalo hunters and skinners headed out to Indian country.

They hauled about 30 wagons full of supplies. They stopped about a mile northeast of Bent's old trading post known as Adobe Walls. That's where Kit Carson had fought against Indians in 1844.

Charlie Myers built a 30 by 60 foot picket store (made of small logs). Tom O'Keefe put up a 15 by 15 picket blacksmith shop south of Myers. Jim Hanrahan made a 25 by 60 foot sod house saloon south of O'Keefe. Charles Rath, another Dodge City businessman, arrived a little later and put up a sod house store south of Hanrahan. Myers also built a 200 by 200 foot picket corral that cornered on his building. Those buildings made up the new settlement of Adobe Walls (though no walls were adobe).

Meanwhile Billy Dixon continued to hunt buffalo. He ventured south of the Adobe Walls settlement. The further south he went, the more dangerous it was. But that was where most remaining buffalo were.

By June rumors flew about Indians banding together for a possible raid on the settlement. Some knew more than rumors. Death began to stalk some of the hunters. Small bands of Indians did what they could to discourage invaders in their territory.

Tom Wallace and Dave Dudley were killed on Chicken Creek while their partner was trading at Adobe Walls. Hunters John

"Antelope Jack" Holmes, an Englishman, and Blue Billy, a German, were killed on a tributary of the Salt Fork of the Red River.

This was enough for Billy Dixon. He began hunting north of Adobe Walls. By then he had a reputation as a prolific hunter for good reason. He could bring down a buffalo from a half mile away, maybe more. Often it was hard for skinners to keep up with him.

By the middle of June some of the merchants at Adobe Walls found out about a possible Indian raid on Adobe Walls. They were reluctant to share the news. One of the founders of Dodge City, Robert M. Wright, was a partner with Charles Rath. So Wright had special interest in the success of Adobe Walls. When he found out news of a specific threat to the settlement, he warned Rath but hoped others wouldn't find out.

Meanwhile hundreds of Comanches, Kiowas, and Cheyennes had banded together to get rid of the Adobe Walls invaders. These Indians believed Adobe Walls threatened their very existence. The Indians decided to attack on June 27. When Wright found this out from secret informants, he relayed the information to Rath, and Rath informed Hanrahan and Myers.

These men along with John and Wright Mooar, major buffalo traders in the area, kept this to themselves. They were afraid hunters would desert the settlement if they had any idea of a raid.

A couple of days before the attack the Mooar brothers left for Dodge City. Shortly after that Charles Rath and Charlie Myers also headed out. For some reason Tom O'Keefe was never told of the danger. That left Jim Hanrahan as the only one at Adobe Walls who had any idea of the possible disaster.

But even Hanrahan couldn't be sure. When he saw the others who knew about the danger leaving, though, he got the jitters. What if it did happen? What could Hanrahan do to prevent a slaughter without looking like the boy who cried wolf? The total population at Adobe Walls was 28 men and one woman. If hundreds of Indians attacked without warning, he could imagine how fast they would be wiped out.

On June 26, Hanrahan had an idea. He waited till two a.m., then fired his pistol.

Several woke up startled. Hanrahan yelled, "Clear out, the ridge pole is breaking!" This got some attention. Someone used a forked pole to prop up the ridgepole though no one could see a break in it. Hanrahan then offered free drinks to those who would stay awake.

Accounts for years said providence of a cracking ridgepole left most in the settlement awake. Providence came in the form of Jim Hanrahan.

At pre-dawn some 700 Indians encouraged by Quahadi Comanche medicine man Isatai ("Little Wolf") and led by Chief Quanah Parker attacked. They rode in from the east. When Billy Dixon realized the danger he reached for his Sharps buffalo rifle and began firing.

The battle raged. Two hunters, Ike and Shorty Shadler, who had camped outside Charlie Myer's picket corral, were killed and scalped in the first attack. They were the only victims that first day.

The hunters' buffalo rifles proved more deadly than the Indians expected. Several times Indians discussing their next move at a distance were shot from their horses.

The second day Billy Dixon proved his reputation didn't exceed his abilities. He aimed his Sharps rifle at one of the raiders who sat on his horse nearly a mile distant (1,538 yards), fired. The bullet found its mark. That along with the continuing barrage of bullets from the buffalo rifles discouraged the attackers beyond hope.

More than 30 of the raiders died in battle. A third buffalo hunter died from a gunshot. And a fourth died from an accidental self-inflicted wound. Eventually the Indians gave up.[1]

◊

Reports throughout southern Kansas and further south increasingly told of Indian raids on farmers and freighters. Between March and July, 1874, hundreds of southern Kansans became frightened enough to leave the state. The stories were not all rumors though newspapers hoped they were.

Reports came in from northern, western, and southern Kansas. A Topeka paper told of some of these incidents. In June it said:

"Our correspondent at Hutchinson sends the following statement in detail of the recent Indian raid in Barbour and Comanche counties. This information was obtained by our correspondent from Mr. Charles Collins, sheriff of Reno County, and is without doubt the most correct version of the affair yet published. He says:

"The first outbreak of the Indians was on Mule creek, in Comanche County. It appears that about a dozen of them, supposed to be Cheyennes, made an attempt to stampede the stock and thereby run it off, but were prevented in this by the mail carrier, H. P. Trustal.

"They next went to Kiowa, where they ran off about twelve head of horses and fired into the houses, wounding two persons. From there they followed up Medicine Lodge River, and about four miles south of town they overtook a farmer by the name of Kime, who had been to the town of Medicine Lodge. They shot and scalped him and left him dead in his wagon, taking his horses.

"They then started in a westward direction, and after proceeding a few miles, came upon two men at work getting out posts. Both were shot and scalped. It appears from the position in which these two men were lying, they must have been shot while at work. From there they [the Indians] escaped to the Indian Territory with about 25 head of horses.

"The same day another party of Indians, about 45 in number, attacked two men at the head of Mule creek, who were there locating a stock ranch. The Indians killed and scalped them both. The men were well armed with needle guns, and from the number of shells (or blank cartridges) around them, they must have made a desperate resistance.

"Five men in all were killed and scalped in the neighborhood of Medicine Lodge. There is a rumor that seven more have met the same fate.

"At the present time everybody in and around Medicine Lodge is in the town and fortifying it with a view of protecting themselves from the threatening attacks of the Indians. Their crops, stock, and much other valuable property have been left to the mercy of the Indians. Their crops, I am informed, look well and prosperous, but unless aid can be sent them soon, the cattle and hogs [running wild] will destroy [the crops]...

"The citizens have barely sufficient supplies to last them five days, and are poorly furnished with arms and ammunition. The opinion is that unless they are aided by men, arms, and provisions, they will be compelled to leave the country.

"In a little town called Kiowa, about 12 miles below Medicine Lodge, there are about 25 families who have left their farms and built a stockade and are all living in it.

In . . . Sun City, [citizens] have also built a stockade, and all the people in that vicinity are living in it—they are also in a very destitute condition. There is a company of 40 men already formed by Dr. Flick, in Hutchinson, who are now ready at a moment's warning to go to the assistance of Medicine Lodge."

The article suggested a remedy. It came from the people themselves.

"It is the general sentiment here that the Indians ought to be brought to a speedy account, and that by force of arms. There can be any number of men obtained in the border counties who will volunteer to go. All the people ask is to be armed with proper orders to clear the country of these lawless bands. I am informed that the Indian agents have been apprized of the fact that the Indians were going on the warpath for the last thirty days, and have failed to give any notice to the settlers of it."[2]

That incident reflected the situation throughout the southern plains. It had been building up for several years. Indians increasingly attacked settlers, freighters, traders, and cattlemen.

These Native Americans saw their world crumbling. Buffalo increasingly disappeared. More and more Indians entered reservations. Those on reservations left whenever they could to hunt and increasingly raid and kill settlers.

Indian agents, usually Quakers (Society of Friends), believed all problems between settlers and Indians had a peaceful solution. They tended to overlook any violence as accidental or excusable. Settlers saw it radically otherwise.

By spring and summer 1874 this problem turned into a crisis. Enough reports of fighting and bloodshed reached Major General William Sherman, who was in command of the Army west of the Mississippi, for him to treat it seriously. After convincing Secretary of War William Belknap that the situation called for desperate measures, Sherman sent a message to General Philip Sheridan, who served under Sherman. The July 20, 1874 message told Sheridan to turn the troops loose on the Indians, which meant for Sheridan to do whatever it took to quell the Indian raids throughout the southern plains.[3] This order marked the beginning of the Red River War in the Texas staked plains, which continued throughout 1874 and into 1875.

◊

Shortly before the Army entered this War, though, people in southern Kansas sought their own way to deal with this problem. Towns formed small militias to protect citizens from the roaming bands of Indians.

In Caldwell, panic sat in on Saturday afternoon, July 4th when a courier came there saying 500 Indians were on a rampage only five miles away from town. Some believed him, others didn't. But a second report from Indian Territory clinched it for many.

On Monday afternoon, July 6th a four-horse stagecoach entered Caldwell. On it were John D. Miles, head of the Cheyenne-Arapaho Agency in Darlington, and his family. When Miles stepped off the stage, he told townspeople what had happened near Bull Foot Station some 70 miles south of Caldwell. J.C. and Lou Hopkins, proprietors of the Pond Creek Station in Indian Territory, were also on the stage.

On his way north from the Cheyenne Agency (110 miles south of Caldwell) Miles came to a burning wagon near Bull Foot Station (about 40 miles from the agency). The smoldering wagon belonged to Pat Hennessey, who along with at least two other freighters, had been murdered and burned. Hennessey was tied to the wheels of the wagon.

Miles knew Indians were raiding settlers and this confirmed it for him. But he blamed freighters, traders, and horse thieves for pushing Indians into this behavior. Traders brought alcohol and guns, and horse thieves stole the Indians' horses.

Miles' warning to Caldwell of imminent danger put many townspeople in real panic. Some began building defenses while others retreated to nearby rivers to hide. Much of the livestock ran free as the settlers prepared for the "onslaught."

Miles stopped in Caldwell long enough to warn of an attack. Then he and his family continued north. Miles was on his way to report the Indian problem to his superiors in Leavenworth.

Miles' warning spread like wildfire. Joe Thralls recalled the warning reaching Wellington.

"At two o'clock in the morning of July 6 [7?], a little sawed-off freighter by the name of Fletcher rode into Wellington yelling 'Indians' at every jump of his horse and appealing for men and arms to defend Caldwell against the anticipated attack," Thralls said.[4]

Sheriff John G. Davis did what he could with those available. He formed a citizens' militia. Thralls' memory placed the number at 21. Others thought there were fewer.

Bill Hackney remembered many said they would join but few did. "We called a meeting and I counted out 150 to go with me to [Caldwell's] relief, telling them to be back in half an hour," he said. "When the time was up only ten men appeared, among them, I remember, were Joe Thralls and Capt. Myers."

Among the militiamen who went with Sheriff Davis were Joe Thralls and brother Elsie, Bill Hackney, C. S. Brodbent, A. W.

Sherman, L. K. Myers, J. A. Kirk, T. J. Riley, James Stipp, John H. Folks, and several others. This group soon headed to Caldwell to help strengthen the defenses. As they rode southwest to Caldwell, they met large groups of settlers fleeing northeast in mortal fear of an Indian attack.

When Joe Thralls, then a constable, arrived in Caldwell early that morning, he sized up the situation. He didn't like what he saw, but it didn't have to do with Indians.

. "The Indian scare had driven most of the horse thieves operating down in the Territory into Caldwell," he said. "They were worse than the Indians and when we found a bunch of them eating breakfast at Caldwell it made us want to turn the Indian hunt into a horse-thief capturing expedition."[5]

A correspondent for the Topeka paper described the situation in Caldwell similarly. "The country around here is full of horse thieves, the town of Caldwell and the timber of Bluff Creek being a sort of refuge for them," he said. "Bully Brooks, formerly of Dodge City, and a number of ruffians of that kidney, have been driven in from the Territory by fear of Indians..."[6]

Within a few days, Wichita, located 30 miles north of Wellington, felt the same panic. They formed a militia as quickly as possible. "The militia company is officered as follows, the officers being elected by vote at a meeting [July 10th]," said the Topeka paper. The officers included "S. M. Tucker, captain; Mike Meagher, 1st lieutenant; and Cash Henderson, 2nd lieutenant. Mr. Tucker is an old soldier, formerly a resident of Fort Scott, and now a practicing lawyer in this city. Mike Meagher is a famous scout in the southwest, formerly marshal of Wichita, and a terror to the long-haired, pistol-shooting gentry from Texas and the Territory. Mr. Henderson is a salesman in a dry goods store in this city, but a good man for the position notwithstanding the peaceful character of his occupation."[7]

Before leaving Wellington with their militia, Joe Thralls borrowed a "three-band Sharps needle gun" from his friend Frank

Bates, who owned a hardware store.[8] Thralls took along a belt full of cartridges just in case they ran into trouble.

That morning a scout rode into Caldwell from the south saying there were no Indians anywhere near the border. Thralls and the others welcomed that news. But their work was not finished. They wanted at least to check out the situation in Indian Territory first hand. And as they ate breakfast, they observed another unfolding crisis.

J.C. and Lou Hopkins, proprietors of the Pond Creek Station between the Cheyenne agency and Caldwell, had also heard the news from the scout. The Hopkins had come to Caldwell after rumors of Indian raids had reached their station. Others back at the station had set up defenses, but were short on guns. The Hopkins brothers hoped to remedy that by stocking up on supplies, including weapons and ammunition, and hauling them back. Now that it sounded like the coast was clear, they packed up and left.

Joe Thralls and the other militiamen watched as the Hopkins left. Joe had talked to the Hopkins when the militiamen first arrived in Caldwell and he knew their situation. Now he became apprehensive. The Hopkins brothers could have trouble defending themselves from two sources. Besides rampaging Indians, there was the added danger from horse thieves. It wasn't that J.C and Lou were tenderfoots but they could easily be outnumbered.

A short time after the Hopkins left town, Thralls noticed the behavior of eight of the shady characters in town. These men, after finishing their breakfast, mounted horses and rode south.

Thralls had an idea what those men were up to. "We believed that it was the intention of these thieves to kill the Hopkins brothers, run off their stock, loot the store, and then charge the crime up to the Indians," he said.[9]

That clinched it. The Wellington party had come to protect citizens and now it looked like citizens needed protecting, specifically the Hopkins. The Wellington militia group, except for Folks, followed after the suspected horse thieves hoping to prevent bloodshed.

"After a brisk ride we caught up with the thieves, who were riding a short distance behind the two Hopkins brothers," Thralls remembered. "When we rode up they stopped and were apparently holding a conference, but they followed on after our party. We caught up with the Hopkins brothers, who were mighty glad to see us, for they had also guessed that the purpose of the thieves was to murder them."[10]

From that point on the militiamen stayed with the Hopkins. The suspected horse thieves rode close by. All the riders continued south, wary of each other. According to Thralls, they continued on till they reached Polecat ranch, where they stopped to give the horses a break to eat grass for a couple of hours.

This gave the "horse thieves" a chance to mingle with the militiamen. Their job of escorting the Hopkins brothers was just about over and Thralls and the others were just about to turn around and head back to Caldwell. The suspected horse thieves, headed by the Moore brothers, according to Bill Hackney, planned to continue riding south. They took this time as an opportunity to obtain something they wanted – the Sharps rifle Thralls carried.

"A gun of that kind was a very valuable asset in those days, although dangerous at both ends when fired," said Thralls. "The thieves coveted this gun so much that they were willing at one time to measure strength with our party to get it. They even demanded it, and finally said that if we didn't give it up, they would take it just the same."[11]

Bill Hackney remembered the "thieves" had a ready-made reason for wanting the guns. "The leader of the gang of the Moore Brothers told me they were going on a dangerous trip and had nothing but revolvers and wanted our guns, stating they would send them back when they got to Fort Sill."[12]

At first Joe Thralls politely refused to give up the Sharps needle gun since he had borrowed it from his friend. But that didn't satisfy the gang leader. Then Hackney offered a compromise. He told the gang they could borrow some of the other guns but not the one Thralls had.

This didn't satisfy the gang leader. He headed back across the road to tell his partners, who were drinking and waiting for the guns. They didn't like what they heard. Hackney remembered how one particular member of the gang responded.

"A great big Texan jumped up and said, 'Hell, what's the use of bothering with them? Let's take that gun and the others.'"

While the bickering heated up, some of the militiamen had anticipated what might follow. So they secretly prepared for action. "Seeing the storm approaching and sensing the real character of these men, some of us had quietly left the circle and laid hold of our guns fully expecting a tragedy," said C.S. Brodbent.[13]

As the gang walked over to the militiamen ready to grab the guns and leave, Bill Hackney had a different idea. According to Joe Thralls it surprised the gang.

"Everybody was ready on our side for them to open the ball," said Thralls, "when Bill Hackney, who then was in his prime, opened up on the thieves in characteristic Hackney style.

"I have heard Bill cuss a good many times, but never heard him do as artistic a job as he did that day. The rest of us were no mollycoddles, but Bill's language almost made us shudder. In substance, Bill spoke as follows: 'If you ---- sons of ------- want that gun, come and get it, but I want to say that if one of you makes a move in that direction, there will be a lot of dead horse thieves left here on the ground for buzzard feed.'

"Bill's defiance had its effect," Thralls added. "The thieves looked Bill and the rest of the party over and decided that the job was too dangerous. Had the fight commenced we might have lost some of our party, but that whole bunch of thieves would almost certainly have died, which would have saved a lynching party the trouble of hanging two of them a few days after that on Slate Creek."[14] More than likely the two Thralls referred to were Billy Brooks and Charlie Smith (George Ford).

C.S. Brodbent also remembered the gang's response. He noticed what a powerful affect Bill Hackney's words had on them.

"The effect was instant and wonderful," he said. "All their bravado evaporated. They became docile at once. Few words were spoken. They mounted and rode away."[15]

With that crisis over, Joe Thralls, Bill Hackney, and the rest of the militiamen turned around and headed back to Kansas. They never ran into any Indians their entire time in Indian Territory.

When the Wellington group reached Caldwell on their way home, they noticed many citizens still in a panic. The militiamen got fresh horses in town before leaving. They offered what comfort they could to others, then headed on to Wellington. Between Caldwell and Wellington they met another group of home defenders. They were coming from Belle Plaine to Caldwell to also offer protection to the border town.

"At Chikaskia River we met Col. [H.C.] St. Clair with 120 men coming to our relief," Bill Hackney said. "We explained the situation to them, so they went into camp while we went on to Wellington."

The Belle Plaine group had left their town to a cheering crowd. When they got to Caldwell, people jeered. Caldwell citizens felt the danger was over and believed the Belle Plaine group was grandstanding.

Once the "Indian scare" had passed, Joe Thralls thought he could settle down a more relaxed pace. He had come to enjoy his role as a lawman, but he hoped for less excitement than he'd faced recently.

That year Joe Thralls and his brother Elzy continued in their struggle to pay off their homestead loan and make enough money to get ahead. Both by then had worked at a number of jobs. While Joe spent most of his time as a lawman, he also took on other work. One job may have been with C.E. Trowbridge's implement company. Elzy occasionally traveled to Indian Territory to buy horses, bring them back to Wellington, and sell them at a profit.

Life returned to normal for a while – that is, for about a week. Then Joe faced a challenge that would dwarf what he had just gone through.

5

"This is the beginning of the end."

The Indian scare in early July 1874 temporarily distracted southern Kansas settlers from another problem – horse thief gangs. These gangs pulled off some major horse and mule stealing in the area shortly before the scare and were glad for some relief from attention.

On Monday, June 29, a band of horse thieves stole eight mules and two horses from Vail and Company, a stage line that had recently outbid the South Western Stage Company for carrying mail between Caldwell, Kansas and Fort Sill, Indian Territory. Vail and Company was scheduled to begin driving its route in July.

Pat Hennessey was killed on July 4th. That's when people panicked and volunteer militiamen joined together to protect others. That gave the horse thieves time to cover their tracks. Soon the stage agent L.T. Williamson offered a $300 reward for the return of the animals.

By July it became obvious southern Kansas faced a drought. Crops dried up. One blistering day followed another. No rain fell between June and August. Though Thralls lived in Wellington, he still tried to maintain a homestead east of there (the southwest 160 acre quarter section from Seneca and the Oxford Road, now U.S. 160).

That year he tried to raise some corn. The drought stunted its growth. The corn never got more than shoulder high. On August

5th grasshoppers invaded, cleaning out the stunted corn. According to Thralls, all that remained after the grasshoppers left was some prairie grass and bluestem.[1]

On July 15, 1874, news reached lawmen in Sumner County about the location of some horse thieves who were traveling north from Indian Territory. The news reached Constable Joe Thralls only days after he returned from Indian Territory where he confronted the suspected horse thieves who wanted his borrowed Sharps rifle. Also Thralls and his brother Elsie still struggled to maintain their homestead.

So Joe and his fellow lawmen had little time for rest. When news on the whereabouts of horse thieves came, Joe had mixed feelings. He'd hoped to rest up from the recent journey. But he was also glad for a chance to catch horse thieves.

The information came from A.C. McLean, who ran the Last Chance/ First Chance trader's ranch and saloon. The Last Chance was located one mile south of Caldwell at a loop in Bluff Creek. Cowboys and outlaws coming and going between Indian Territory and Kansas often stopped at the ranch. So McLean often ran across outlaws on the move.

McLean later claimed he heard about the horse thieves during the Indian scare. McLean said Burr Mosier at Buffalo Springs station (63 miles south of Caldwell) asked him to come down and help families at the station move to a safer place.

When McLean arrived at Baker's Skeleton Creek ranch (47 miles south of Caldwell) on the way, Jasper "Granger" Marion, part of the horse thief ring, told McLean about his encounter with Indians. When Marion and William Watkins, a fellow horse thief, ran from attacking Indians, Marion escaped but Watkins was killed and the Indians took the horse he was riding. The horse happened to be one the thieves recently stole. The horse thieves still held at least six mules and two horses, hiding them near Mosier's ranch on Turkey Creek. Marion also told McLean that the thieves would get $600 from the Southwestern Stage Company for stealing the animals from Vail and Company.[2]

McLean had owned and run a traders ranch at least since 1871. That year, the busiest in the history of trail driving, he and a partner ran a trader's ranch on the north bank of the Ninnescah River where the Chisholm Trail crossed. When McLean got back to Caldwell, he told Dr. J.M. Burkett, a Caldwell druggist, about the thieves. Burkett told A.M. Colson, a Caldwell town leader. On Wednesday, July 15, Colson rode north to the Chikaskia River area, where the horse thieves had stolen horses from the settlers. There he had no trouble finding recruits. Then he headed south to Fall River to pick up a couple more. Sometime after Colson heard the news, he telegraphed Sheriff John G. Davis in Wellington for help.

Colson's group included Frank Barrington, Alexander Williamson, Bob Drummond, a man named Force, John Williams, and A. Livingston from the Chikaskia River area along with Ballard Dixon and George Peringer from Fall River. That night Colson's posse got lost. They decided to stop for sleep and start in the morning when they could see where they were going. In the morning they headed north.[3] In the morning Dixon and Peringer went home.

Meanwhile Sheriff Davis' chose the best he could find in Wellington. This included township constable Joe Thralls; Thomas C. Gatliff, a Wellington grocer who later served as town marshal; John Botkin, a farmer; and two others, Stevenson and Abrell. Stevenson may have been R.W. Stevenson, who served as a deputy sheriff and Abrell may have been R.W. Abrell who had been fined for disturbing the peace in November 1873.[4]

The Davis posse rode south to the Caldwell area where Davis rendezvoused secretly with a contact there about the horse thieves. Then the posse rode north into a storm and had to stop for the night. Next morning they rode till they met up with the Colson party at Andrew Drumm's ranch in the Chikaskia River area.

"Major" Drumm was a prominent cattleman known throughout Kansas and later Oklahoma who became a leading figure in the Cherokee Strip Live Stock Association. A one-time California gold miner from Zanesville, Ohio, Drumm drove a herd of cattle from Texas to Kansas in 1870. From then on he maintained a consuming interest in the cattle business. He loved the excitement, the risk, the challenge, and the change from his previous work.

Drumm eventually owned 150,000 cattle with partner Andy Snyder at their ranch in the Cherokee Strip. According to Paul Wellman, Drumm became the first cattle grower to settle in the Cherokee Strip and later became the first big rancher to put up barbed wire.[5]

Major Drumm typified the adventurous spirit of those who traveled west in the 19th century. He enjoyed the risks involved, gambling his life on an unknown future. Once out west he also gambling for money and property.

Newspaperman Tom McNeal, who knew Drumm, told of the time Drumm played a game of poker with a Texan. Their stakes were cattle and land. "When the cards were laid upon the table," said McNeal, "Major Drumm had three aces and the Texas gentleman had three jacks. As the result of the game, Drumm theoretically placed in his hip pocket 750 steers, a large number of blooded bulls, a considerable herd of one and two-year-old heifers and cows of high and low degree, ten mustangs, and a ranch in the panhandle of Texas."[6]

At Drumm's ranch by the Chikaskia River, both Sheriff Davis' Wellington party and A.M. Colson's party, now joined as one, ate breakfast and heard the latest news from the rancher. Drumm had good reason to help the posse. He didn't like the idea of horse or cattle thieves roaming around his ranch and possibly practicing their skills on his property.

Soon the joint posse finished breakfast and headed out to continue their chase after the horse thieves. They headed west till they came to H.J. Devore's ranch about 12 miles west of Caldwell. But in their effort to get organized, they lost valuable time. They heard the latest news about the thieves from someone at the ranch. The thieves had passed by a day earlier riding a wagon and trailing mules and horses. They were headed north.

The horse thieves had stayed on the move during the Indian scare. After hiding the mules and horses at Turkey Creek near Burr Mosier's Buffalo Springs ranch for awhile, the thieves had moved the animals to the Pole Cat (now Renfrow) about 12 miles south of Caldwell.

It now seemed they were headed northwest, perhaps for Larned or Dodge City, or Colorado. Most of the posse suspected the thieves were headed to the Larned-Dodge City area to a trader's ranch. This ranch was located about 2 ½ to three miles east of Fort Larned. Run by Albert Henry Boyd, a member of the town company that founded Larned, the Boyd ranch also often entertained outlaws.

Boyd, who founded the ranch in 1868, had a saloon there to attract traveling traders and cowboys. The ranch was located where the Santa Fe Trail crossed Pawnee Creek. Boyd also couldn't pass up the chance for extra money made from fees charged from people using his crudely constructed toll bridge across Pawnee Creek. Boyd seemed to have every angle covered for making money at his otherwise remote location.

The main ranch building, made of sod, was about 20 feet wide by 40 feet long. A hallway passed through the length of it going north and south. The saloon was at the southwest corner and a room for saddles and guns at the southeast corner. To the north of these rooms were rows of small sleeping rooms (perhaps cribs for prostitutes).

If the law were ever to catch up with the suspected horse thieves, this was the time. The posse hoped to catch them before they could find shelter around Larned.

Trailing the suspected outlaws soon proved a greater challenge than the posse anticipated. Kansas then was in the middle of a severe drought. The longer the posse rode, the hotter and drier they got. In their hurry to follow a hot trail, the posse carried little provisions for any extended search.

Thursday and Friday, July 16 and 17, 1874 the posse continued to ride north hoping to pick up the outlaw trail. Both nights they bedded down without a meal. They found no sign of the outlaws.

Soon some members of the posse dropped out and headed home. Into the third day only half of those who started remained. This included Sheriff Davis, Constable Joe Thralls, Thomas C. Gatliff, John Botkin, and perhaps Meers, all from Wellington; and W.B. King, Frank Barrington, Alexander Williamson, A.M. Colson, John Williams, and Force from the Caldwell area.[7]

This small posse woke early Saturday, July 18, even more determined to find the thieves. So far they had no trail to follow, they hadn't eaten for two days, and they had almost exhausted their supplies. They still suspected the thieves were headed northwest but weren't sure whether to head north or west from where they were in Kingman County. They decided to continue north.

After two stark days, they ran into some luck. They came to a farmhouse, the first inhabited place since leaving the Devore ranch. The farmer befriended them with food, their first meal since Devore's. From the farm the posse decided to turn west and spread out. If their luck held, they might find a trace of the thieves. But luck was against them. They found nothing.

Sunday morning, July 19, still determined, they decided to give it one more try. That day they met a boy driving cattle. They told him about the horse thieves and asked if he saw anyone fitting their description. He had. The thieves had camped on Sand Creek 15 miles to the west the night before.

This gave new life to the hunt. The posse picked up the trail at Sand Creek but had to stop for the night. Monday morning, July 20, they continued following the trail throughout the day. By now everyone in the party was hungry, thirsty, weak, and tired. Their horses dragged along. Neither man nor animal had little energy left.

That afternoon one member shot a jackrabbit. The men roasted it and all shared in the tidbit meal. As evening approached, Sheriff Davis and Thomas Gatliff rode off in search of water. Two miles away they found not only a pond but also remaining embers of wagon bed boards used as fuel by the thieves. Now the posse knew they were only minutes away from the thieves.

At the same time, the posse noticed a settlement nearby. It was Garfield. Four of the famished members rode off to get food there. Two of those left, Sheriff Davis and W.B. King, snuck up a slope to check out any activity in the ravine near them. Soon they spotted the stolen mules and horses as well as two men. They watched helplessly as the two men hitched up a team to the wagon and rode off.

Meantime Williams joined Davis and King. The three men decided they had to do something. They charged into the camp. The posse and the thieves fired at each other. One of the thieves quickly ran off into the Sand Hills. When the thieves fled, they left behind four mules and two horses.

After the rest of the posse returned, Davis led them after the wagon. The posse caught up to it as some of the horse thieves were driving it across the Arkansas River. The posse and the horse thieves fired at each other but no one seemed to stop any lead. The thieves driving the wagon jumped off the wagon and on to horses nearby them and escaped. The posse was left with the wagon and two mules.

Since the posse's horses were played out, Davis figured he and his men had done about all they could to recover the stolen property. On Wednesday, July 22, they headed back with their take.[8]

It took several days' journey for the posse to reach home. When they got to Slate Creek they split up, some heading to Wellington and others to Caldwell. Most of the posse reached home base on Sunday, July 26, 1874.

Their deed did not go unnoticed, especially by L.T. Williamson, head of the Vail and Company Stage Line. The Wellington paper said the $300 reward for recovery of the stage line's animals would go to 11 men: Sheriff John Davis, Thomas C. Gatliff, John Botkin, Joe Thralls, and Meers from Wellington; and Wilder B. "Buffalo" King, Frank H. Barrington, John Williams, A.M. Colson, Alexander Williamson, and Force from around Caldwell.

This reward, the paper added, "will partially repay them for the hardships of the brief campaign. But in addition to this meager reward, the gentlemen will receive the thanks of a grateful people who for years have been compelled to submit to the depredations of this organized band of thieves, by whom they have been mercilessly plundered."[9]

The paper anticipated further action against the horse thief ring. "This is the first successful inroad ever made upon [the horse thief ring]," it said, "and is but the beginning of a short, sharp and decisive campaign by which the power of this organized band of desperadoes is sure to be effectually broken. This is the beginning of the end, but the end is not yet."[10]

L.T. Williamson soon sent a note to Sheriff Davis "containing the warmest expressions of thanks for the services rendered by him and his men in the recovery of the company stock." Williamson enclosed a $300 check to be divided among the posse.[11]

Back in Caldwell, men had organized into vigilance groups determined to catch the horse thieves before they knew about the posse finding the wagon, mules, and horses. The Caldwell vigilantes had decided it was past time to put an end to the horse thief ring.

6

"With Judge Lynch on the bench..."

Sheriff John Davis had no time to rest before word came from Caldwell about warrants issued for the arrest of the leading horse thief suspects. Davis left Wellington Monday afternoon, July 27, 1874 with a few reinforcements.

"Some of the parties for which the warrants had been issued were known to be desperate characters, who were constantly on the look out, and who were always well armed," said the paper. "Understanding this fact, the sheriff summoned to his assistance several of the citizens of Wellington with whom he left for Caldwell."[1]

Joe Thralls more than likely was one of Sheriff Davis' first choices. Again Joe would do what he could to capture outlaws. This time the lawmen received more help from local citizens than they had on the previous chase.

Thralls, then 26, learned much more about his job as a lawman from the recent manhunt. He experienced first hand the frustration of trying to catch lawbreakers and having them escape. He felt what the settlers who were victims of these thieves felt.

In the short time he had been a lawman, he could see how easily outlaws in the West could escape the law. And he began to see how lawbreakers who were caught and went to trial could even then escape justice by manipulating the laws to their advantage.

They hired the best lawyers. But when that was not enough, they paid off others or had their friends on the outside threaten witnesses. And even when these outlaws were convicted of murder, the state of Kansas never executed them, at least not in the 19th century.[2]

Thralls had yet to experience a lynch mob first hand and close up. But he didn't have long to wait.

Sheriff Davis and his small posse stopped outside of Caldwell that evening and waited for information. Soon a scout rode up and talked to Davis. The scout had scoped out the situation in town. He told Davis that the men they were after were well armed and dangerous. If Davis waited a little longer, he would have more people to help him. Davis waited.

Reinforcements from town soon began to gather around Davis. Gradually the sheriff's small posse turned into a crowd. By 2 a.m. there were about 150 to 200 willing and eager citizens ready to follow Davis in their pursuit of the suspected horse thieves.

Davis directed these vigilantes to spread out and surround Caldwell as best they could. The vigilantes were looking for six men: L. Ben Hasbrouck, William L. "Bully" Brooks, "One Armed" Charlie Smith (George Ford), Judson H. "Judd" Calkins, Dave Terrill, and A.C. McLean. Warrants had been issued for all but Charlie Smith and Dave Terrill.

L. Ben Hasbrouck was Caldwell's first lawyer. He was described as "a young lawyer, about 22 years of age, and considered the most handsome young man in this country. He had been educated in the city of New York, and not only had more than usual ability as an attorney, but possessed those qualities which are requisite in any young man in order to make him a gentleman of the first class."[3]

His trouble in Caldwell started in late 1872, when he was accused of stealing. His court case dragged out for eight months, ending on August 15, 1873. The Belle Plaine paper reported it as follows:

"The most important case tried at this term of the District Court was the State of Kansas vs. L.B. Hasbrouck – a lawyer of Caldwell,

66

in this county - who was charged with stealing a cow on or about the 16th day of December 1872, said cow being then and there the property of one Seymore Dye. The prosecution was conducted by C. Wilsie, Judge McDonald and Judge Adams. Mr. Hasbrouck [was defended] by himself, W.C. Doncarlos and Judge Blodgett. The case was well conducted upon both sides by the distinguished counsel in charge, and considerable feeling manifested by both prosecuting witnesses, defense and attorneys. The jury after hearing the arguments retired to their room at nine o'clock P.M. on the 14th [of August, 1873], and at ten o'clock the next day returned into court with their verdict, which read as follows: 'We the jury in this cause [sic] find that the plaintiff [sic] is not guilty.'"[4]

Though Hasbrouck was found not guilty, Caldwell citizens continued to believe he not only stole the cow, but also headed up a band of horse thieves. Yet they could never prove it.

William "Bully" Brooks by 1874 had a checkered past. In the last two years he had stumbled into jobs from one place to another. None of the jobs had lasted long.

Back in 1872 Brooks had become Newton, Kansas' first city marshal. He gained a reputation as a belligerent troublemaker who liked to dominate others. Some called him "Bully" rather than "Billy" behind his back. They didn't want to stop one of his bullets by saying it to his face.

On June 9, 1872 his career and life nearly ended. Two Texas cowboys, James Hunt and Joe Miller, were making trouble in a Newton dance hall when Bully Brooks showed up. He ordered the cowboys to leave town. They started to but then wheeled around and shot him. Brooks stopped a bullet in his collarbone and two more in his limbs before the cowboys left. Brooks then jumped on his horse and chased them for 10 miles. Brooks soon recovered from his wounds.

He left Newton shortly after that. He went to Ellsworth, briefly served as a policeman, then moved to Dodge City. There he developed a reputation as a buffalo hunter. Some called him "Buffalo Bill."

Soon he was embroiled in another fight. Though he was no longer a lawman, he still liked to use his gun. On December 23, 1872 he argued with a Santa Fe Railroad yardmaster named Brown. The argument turned violent. Brown and Brooks both pulled out their guns. Each fired three times. Brown's first bullet hit Brooks, wounding him. Brooks' third shot grazed a bystander and pierced Brown's body, killing him instantly.

Five days later, on Saturday, December 28, 1872 Brooks fought again. This time it was against Dodge City saloonkeeper Matthew Sullivan. They had become enemies and this day Brooks decided to end the bickering by ending Sullivan's life. Sullivan was minding his saloon business when someone stuck a gun through an open window and shot him dead. Most believed the culprit was Brooks but no one could prove it.

Two months later, on March 4, 1873 Brooks argued with a buffalo hunter named Kirk Jordan. Again, it turned violent. Their fistfight proved nothing. But Jordan wasn't about to forget the incident. Later that day Jordan spotted Brooks in the street. Jordan raised his buffalo rifle and fired. In that split second, Brooks leaped behind a water barrel. The bullet pierced the two barrels and hit an iron hoop.

The next day Brooks stayed on his best behavior. He even went to Jordan and patched up their differences. Then he left town permanently.

Since then Brooks became a familiar figure around Caldwell. He frequented the traders' ranches from the Indian Territory into Kansas. He acquired the reputation of a horse thief. As mentioned earlier, people had noticed him in Caldwell around other suspected horse thieves during the recent Indian scare.

He lived in a dugout about a half-mile outside of town, according to Mrs. Jacob B. Rideout, wife of Caldwell's Presbyterian minister. "He had lived at Caldwell but a short time," Rideout said, "and was doubtless a bad man. He was very large, and about 30 years of age. [On Monday, July 27] he was in town with a rifle looking for another desperado that he might kill him. At the same time the other was lurking around and dodging from place to place seeking an opportunity to kill Brooks."[5]

"One Armed Charlie" Smith also had a well-developed reputation. His real name was probably George Sewell Ford. He was a son of Thomas Ford (born December 5, 1800; died November 3, 1850), former Illinois Supreme Court justice (1841-42) and governor (1842-46) who had Ford County, Illinois named after him. Charlie's younger brother, alias Tom Smith, had been lynched in 1872 for stealing a horse from Milton Freeman. Tom Smith was believed to be part of a horse thief ring working for Curley Marshall, original owner of the Last Chance ranch and saloon south of Caldwell. People from Tom Smith's hometown always believed he was innocent of the crime.[6]

"Charlie Smith" (George Ford) came from Illinois to run a traders' ranch on the Ninnescah River (somewhere near present day Clearwater) in 1870. He lost the lower part of his right arm in a shooting accident in 1871. By 1872 G.D. Freeman said Smith made the Last Chance his headquarters, often traveled to Wichita, and was considered a "gentleman of leisure."[7] Smith was believed to be part of the horse thief ring around Caldwell. Again Mrs. Rideout had her own view of Charlie Smith-George Ford. By 1874 he was "very much degraded on account of strong drink... During the previous winter he sat day after day in front of the saloons dressed in the same old brown suit. His hair was long and matted. He slept wherever night found him... He was so completely under the influence of whiskey and so thoroughly controlled by bad men that he would not listen to any words of friendly counsel..."[8]

Judd Calkins owned a livery barn in Caldwell. According to G.D. Freeman and Mrs. Rideout, he also ran the City Hotel. Four of the stolen mules had been taken from Calkins' barn.

Dave P. Terrill was a saloonkeeper in early Caldwell. Curley Marshall sold the Last Chance to Terrill in 1871. Though A.C. McLean owned the Last Chance in 1874, Terrill's close association with that saloon as well as suspected horse thieves brought him under suspicion.

A.C. McLean, present owner of the Last Chance, also had close ties to a number of shady characters. He lived a mile south of town. Mrs. Rideout described him as "a large fleshy man, but crippled with rheumatism. He had kept a dance house [Last Chance Saloon], but it was burned by the citizens and he had barely escaped with his life."[9]

The vigilantes closed in on the suspects. One by one they tracked them down.

The vigilantes found Hasbrouck in a cornfield. They found Calkins at the City Hotel. They found Dave Terrill three miles northwest of town at the home of J.L. "Deacon" Jones. Jones had been Terrill's partner when Terrill got his first saloon.

They found McLean at his home near the Last Chance. When they entered the house, McLean's wife said he was sick in bed. This didn't detract the vigilantes from their mission. They told Mrs. McLean that he had to go to Wellington sick or well.

The only suspect who offered any resistance was Billy Brooks. He was holed up in his dugout a half-mile south of town. The paper said there were two men with him and "Bill Brooks, after several hours siege, came out of his fortification and delivered his arms to the sheriff."[10] Mrs. Rideout, who knew Mrs. Brooks, said Brook's wife was with him and recounted the following dialogue during the siege.

"Sheriff Davis: Come out and give yourself up like a man.

"Brooks: You'll never take me alive.

"Davis: If you give yourself up, I'll defend you from the mob and you'll have a fair trial.

"Brooks: I'll never get to Wellington alive.

"Davis: I have control of my men and if you give yourself up, I pledge my word you'll have a fair trial.

"Brooks: I know the mob will hang me and I'll not give myself up alive. If you take me, you'll take me a dead man. But I'll sell my life as dearly as possible.

"Davis: I'll give you 10 minutes to send your wife out of the dugout.

"Brooks: My wife will assist me, so proceed as soon as you like.
"Davis: Send your wife out and we'll let her depart in peace. I don't wish to fight a woman.
"Brooks: My wife will not leave. She is a better warrior than you or any of the men you have in your crowd.
"Davis: You're foolish to lose your own life and endanger the life of your wife rather than defend yourself before an honorable court with the probability of being set at liberty.
"Brooks: I'm not afraid of an honorable court, but I understand mob law too well to expect any such thing as [being set free] should I give myself up as a prisoner today. So I shall not throw myself into the hands of a mob, but I don't object to dying here. I have the advantage and will sell my life as dearly as possible.
"Davis: I have 200 men and it will not take long to bring you out.
"Brooks: I know, but you will exchange a good many lives for mine. I'm all ready, so go right ahead without any more talk."
At this point Brook's wife told him not to give up. But then one of Brook's old acquaintances outside called out, "You're perfectly safe in surrendering. The sheriff tells me there's no danger. I'll go with you to Wellington and see that you're not harmed."[11]
Brooks believed his friend. He walked out of the dugout into Davis' custody. Davis' group rode to Wellington. Mrs. Brooks walked the 25 miles from Caldwell to Wellington that same day.
Vigilantes still didn't have Charlie Smith. He headed south into Indian Territory when he figured out vigilantes were after him. Some of the vigilantes eventually caught up with him and brought him back in time for him to spend Tuesday night, July 28, in the Wellington jail.
Tuesday afternoon, July 28, Justice James A. Dillar read the charges against Brooks, Hasbrouck, Calkins, and McLean. Dave Terrill was released that afternoon since no warrant had been issued against him. The others were charged with stealing seven mules and with being members of an organized band of thieves. "Charlie Smith" for some reason had no warrant against him, either.

That night the five prisoners got little sleep. They heard angry outbursts from highly charged indignant citizens. They knew the danger they faced. Any moment a crowd of vigilantes might break through the guards and take them away. They may have been surprised to find they had survived the first night.

Calkins and McLean found themselves also lucky the next day. Calkins was released on bond ("$500 straw bail" according to Sumner County Press). McLean was kept under separate guard and was to be tried on August 5th.

When Terrill and Calkins were released, they went to Dr. P.J.M. Burkett and threatened to kill him, then left. Burkett filed a complaint against them.

Bill Hackney told his own story of Calkins and Terrill's release. He vividly remembered his role in it. He claimed warrants were issued "for the arrest of Judd Calkins, who kept a restaurant at Caldwell [and] Dave Terrell, who kept a livery stable... They were brought to Wellington for trial and put in the calaboose there. Calkins and Terrell were charged, one in his restaurant with feeding bad men and the other, in his livery stable, feeding bad men's horses. They were friends of mine, and while we were in favor of helping the whole outfit, Os Hackney and I decided [vigilantes] should not hang these two men, and while it looked like we probably would go with them, we were obdurate and [the vigilantes] did not hang them."[12]

Mrs. Rideout saw it another way. She said that the three men [Calkins, Terrill, and McLean] asked for two "very able and popular lawyers, who told the prisoners that if they would pay them $100 each, they would set them at liberty. [The three men] were able to raise the amount and so escaped."[13]

As Wednesday dragged on, Brooks, Hasbrouck, and "Smith" nervously stayed in their cell hoping for a further reprieve from angry citizens. Justice Dillar issued new warrants for the arrest of Calkins and Terrill. But it was too late to catch up with them. They were well on their way to Wichita and freedom.

Evening approached. The prisoners bedded down for another night filled with apprehension.

As midnight, July 29, neared, the prisoners heard the rising sound of a crowd outside. It confirmed their worst fears.

Jasper L. Kellogg, a Sumner County pioneer who helped found Belle Plaine and was now the county treasurer, remembered that evening clearly. He and John H. Folks, another early pioneer who edited the *Sumner County Press*, boarded at Sheriff John Davis' house close to the jail. They lived downstairs and Davis lived on the second floor.

"We slept in the front room down stairs and the sheriff was above us," Kellogg said. "About midnight, a party of horsemen surrounded the house and called for Davis. Putting his head out of the window, [Davis] inquired what [they] wanted. They demanded the keys to the calaboose, a block away, ordering him to throw them out, which he promptly did."[14]

The vigilantes rode back to the jail and joined others. There were around 300 in all. They overpowered the guards and used the keys from Davis to enter the cell where Brooks, Hasbrouck, and "Smith" were trapped.

Meantime Kellogg and Folks became curious. They decided to investigate further. They took too long to see the group at the jail. "Captain Folks and I dressed hurriedly and went out onto the street," he said. "The party of 30 or 40 men were then riding off with three horse thieves (Hasbrouck being one) and starting for Slate Creek Bridge. We followed with 20 or 30 spectators, who had heard the racket, but after a few blocks a dozen of the horsemen came charging back ordering us to return. We lost no time in following the suggestion."[15]

Mrs. Rideout felt the same intimidation from the vigilantes. Her husband, Reverend Jacob B. Rideout, wanted to talk one last time to the prisoners before they met their fate. But friends warned him against it.

"It won't do for you to say anything in favor of those men," one told him. "You know a great many of our people have lost their

73

horses and intense excitement prevails." When Rev. Rideout said he still wanted to see the men, his friend told him it would be hopeless since many of the vigilantes were intoxicated. Then the friend played a trick on him. He got him to come to his house, then locked him in and insisted he wait till the trouble was over.[16]

That clear moonlit night, Wednesday, July 29, provided the setting for an eerie scene. "It was a beautiful evening," Mrs. Rideout said. "The moon shone brightly. Scarcely a cloud could be seen and a gentle southwest breeze added to the enjoyment of such as were seeking recreation by walking in the flowery paths that surrounded the village."

The paper said, "The full moon rose on Wednesday evening, climbing a cloudless sky and smiled down upon a scene of almost unusual quiet. The sound of footfalls of pedestrians on the sidewalks had died away. The villagers had sunk tranquilly to rest, and the doomed prisoners even were sleeping when the ominous tramp, tramp, of marching horsemen broke upon the stillness of the night. And soon emerging from the gloom, approaching from the direction of Slate Creek bridge, could be seen a long line of mounted men preceded by a small body of footmen marching swiftly yet in the most perfect order directly toward that quarter of the town where the prisoners were confined.

"As the head of the column approached the calaboose, the short, sharp cry of 'halt!' rang out upon the stillness of the night and the click of carbines was heard. For a single moment the column halted when 50 horsemen broke from the ranks and instantly surrounded the calaboose, dismounted, disarmed the guards and possessed themselves of the key [or at least used the key they got from Sheriff Davis]. The doors were thrown open and the prisoners brought out with their hands securely bound.

"During all this time not a word was spoken. The silence was oppressive.

"The three doomed men, with ropes about their necks, were taken in charge by the squad of footmen who placed themselves in a square, formed by the cavalry, and in this order they marched in the direction of Slate Creek bridge. Everything thus far was done quietly and with the utmost precision and celerity. Not even a dog barked and the slumbers of the nearest families were not disturbed."[17]

The vigilantes went about a mile south of Wellington on the road to Caldwell before they came to a particular tree by the creek. There they stopped and looped the three ropes around one branch.

L.B. Hasbrouck asked for permission to talk before the vigilantes lynched him. They said no but he said he felt faint. He asked for a drink of water. Someone went to the creek, filled a hat, and brought it to him. He drank, then said, "Boys, let me go and I will leave the place and never return. You will never hear from me again." A few of the vigilantes sympathized with him. But it did no good. The vigilante leaders looped the rope around Hasbrouck's neck. He then said, "My life is of no account, but don't ever let my parents know what became of me. It would break their hearts."[18]

Brooks, according to G.D. Freeman, pleaded for his life while his wife watched, helpless. "Charlie Smith" acted like he had no regrets.

The vigilantes strung them up next to each other on the one branch of the tree. Hasbrouck was lynched furthest out on the limb and about 20 feet from the ground. Next to him was "One Armed Charlie Smith," and closest to the trunk was Billy Brooks. Brooks' face looked contorted in pain.

The bodies were left hanging till the next morning when they were taken down and laid in the courthouse. Mrs. Brooks knelt down by her dead husband and wept. She later bought a coffin that he was buried in. The other two were buried in rough boxes.

Perhaps never fully explained was A.C. McLean's ability to escape the fate of the other three. He survived the ordeal and took part in his August 5th hearing. It began at 10 a.m. with testimony from P.J.M. Burkett and Burr Mosier before McLean. Both Burkett and Mosier testified in McLean's defense. Burkett said he had known McLean three years and that McLean told Burkett where the stolen animals were but feared for his life if the thieves found out he talked.

Burr Mosier said he'd known McLean 13 years. As early as the first part of July one of the thieves, Jasper "Granger" Marion, told Mosier most of the details about the horse thieves. He mentioned nine thieves. Mosier remembered the names of Hasbrouck, Brooks, "Charlie Smith," Henry Hall, "Red," "Bob," Jerry Williams, and Marion himself. Perhaps Bill Watkins who died in an Indian attack was the ninth. But Mosier insisted McLean had nothing to do with all that. "I do not know anything that would implicate A.C. McLean, the defendant, in the stealing, concealing, or running off of Vail and Company's mules," he said.[19]

Lawmen in Wellington from Sheriff John Davis to City Marshal Dan William Jones and Constable Joe Thralls no doubt knew ahead of time the three horse thief suspects would likely be lynched. Whether they could have stopped it if they'd tried is a moot question. Surely they had mixed feelings, especially Sheriff Davis who had promised Brooks a fair trial.

This was Joe Thralls' first up-close experience of lynch law in Kansas. Late in life he still believed such acts were necessary in early Wild West Kansas.

"It had come to a showdown [as to] who was to run the county, the settlers or the horse thieves," he said. "The settler had his all here and could not leave conveniently; while the thief had only his mount and a pair of Colt's 45's. The south part of the county was organized into vigilance committees or companies.

"There had been many arrests of the thieves and trials in the courts. In almost every case a horde of witnesses were present for the defense when they would prove an alibi and go free. With Judge Lynch on the bench it was different. There were no continuances, no changes of venue. Horse stealing then was a capital offense."

With the situation shaping up the way he explained it, only drastic measures could end the power of horse thieves. Thralls saw the lynchings in 1874 as a major turning point in bringing law and order to southern Kansas. He believed that anything less severe would not have worked.

"None of [the occasional random lynchings] had a deterrent effect on the main body of thieves," he said. "For what did the loss of a few men amount to when there [were] so many of them? But when the citizens of the county got organized and under way, it surely 'put the fear of the Lord in their hearts.'"[20]

7

"Joe Thralls again did his job."

By the middle 1870s cattle drives along the Chisholm Trail to the west of Wellington had died out between Caldwell and towns north such as Abilene, Ellsworth, Newton, and Wichita. Farmers and their crops blocked the way. So did barbed wire. Only Dodge City could claim a healthy cattle business. Caldwell still held out hope if they could get a railroad to build their way. None had so far.

This decline in the cattle trade around Wellington meant less trouble and lawlessness from rowdy cowboys. But it didn't mean the end of crime. The most prevalent crime took a different form. People still took the law in their own hands when they felt like it. Shootings and killings still occurred. And even though the most active horse thief gang in Sumner County was stopped, it didn't mean horse stealing ended.

As 1875 approached, Joe Thralls could look back on two years experience as a lawman. People around Wellington trusted him both in the job he was doing to enforce the law and as a friend ready to help at the drop of a hat. They admired him perhaps more than most others. He had helped track down stolen horses and returned them to the owners. He had willingly headed into Indian Territory at a time when danger seemed to be all around. He had helped squelch spreading outlawry by putting an end to the horse thief ring around Wellington and Sumner County.

Joe and his brother Elzy also successfully farmed on their homestead east of town. Their future looked bright.

But changes took place toward the end of 1874 and beginning of 1875 that discouraged Thralls. He continued to serve as a township constable but other lawmen he knew quit.

Sometime during 1874 Wellington City Marshal Dan W. Jones quit and T. J. Riley briefly took his place.[1] Jones moved to Red Fork Ranch in Indian Territory (now Dover, Oklahoma) on the north bank of the Cimarron River. He still held the position of a deputy U.S. marshal and would continue to serve as such when the need arose. He would later move to Caldwell and become a lawman there. And Joe Thralls would later find himself face to face with Jones on at least one occasion in Thralls' role as sheriff.

While living at Red Fork Ranch, Jones occasionally returned to Wellington for visits. In February 1876 the Wellington paper said, "Dan Jones, formerly of this place, but now keeping a ranch on Red Fork, I.T., was in town several days last week, shaking hands with old friends."

Joe Thralls' close friend Bill Hackney moved from Wellington to Winfield on August 24, 1874.[2] He continued to keep in touch with Thralls and probably was the one who introduced him to another outstanding lawman, Albert T. Shenneman, who lived in Winfield.

In many ways Shenneman's life as a lawman paralleled Joe Thralls'. In the 1880s Thralls would have to deal with a sad event related to Shenneman.

◊

In February 1875 Joe Thralls again headed after horse thieves. "Messrs. [Thomas C.] Gatliff, [Joseph M.] Thralls, and Dunagan [horse thief victim], who left this city in the early part of last week, in pursuit of the thieves who had stolen a span of horses from this last named gentleman, returned last Sunday night [Feb 14]," reported the Wellington paper. "They followed the thieves to within

103 miles of the Texas line, where they lost the trail and had to return without the stock."[3]

Though he wasn't successful, Thralls went well beyond the call of duty. The middle of Indian Territory in 1875 was not the safest and most peaceful spot to be. This was three months before Isaac Parker was appointed judge of the Western District of Arkansas, which would include Indian Territory.

Describing this area during this time, author Glenn Shirley said, "The cattle and horse thief, the prostitute, the desperado, the whiskey peddler – all sought refuge where there was no 'white man's court' and no law under which they could be extradited to the state or territory where they had committed their crimes." Shirley added, "No American frontier ever saw leagues of robbers so desperate, any hands so red with blood. By 1875 this civilization was in the balance. Decent men, red and white alike, cried to the government for protection."[4]

So heading into this area with only one assistant was extremely dangerous. Some would have called it foolhardy. But Joe Thralls saw it as his duty.

◊

Perhaps the greatest change affecting Thralls as a lawman in 1875 came when Sumner County Sheriff John G. Davis resigned. Davis may have had second thoughts about his role as a lawman after the 1874 horse thief gang lynching. He had promised Billy Brooks a fair trial. But when the pressure came, he gave in to the vigilantes, tossing them the keys to the jail. He may have pictured Brooks' wife weeping over Billy Brooks' dead body.

Sheriff Davis thought Joe Thralls would make an excellent replacement. He relayed this to Governor Thomas A. Osborne. Governor Osborne appointed Thralls as the new sheriff on April 19, 1875.

But a few days before that, while Thralls was already acting as sheriff, he carried out part of his duty that got him in hot water. He

81

found out then, as he did several years later, that politics could get him in trouble.

On April 15, 1875, as acting sheriff, he took possession of the *Belle Plaine Democrat* Printing Office and all its contents. The *Belle Plaine Democrat* had ceased publication as a newspaper in 1874.

Democrats were hopping mad. They soon took action. Since Thralls was acting at a time when John G. Davis was no longer sheriff and Thralls had not yet been appointed to replace him, the Democrats figured they had a legal loophole for prosecuting him.

Thus politics played its role. In May the Wellington paper reported what happened. "Joseph Thralls, recently appointed by Governor Osborne [as] sheriff of Sumner County to fill the vacancy created by the resignation and removal of John G. Davis, has been left out in the cold by the refusal of the Commissioners to approve his bond," it said.[5] Thralls resigned as sheriff on May 13, 1875. Two days later Governor Osborne appointed John K. Hastie to replace him.[6]

◊

Thralls returned to his job as township constable. His fellow constable was John A. Kirk. Thomas C. Gatliff served as Wellington city marshal.

On November 2, James E. Reed was elected the next sheriff. Reed appointed J.M. Thralls Under-Sheriff on January 1, 1876 but revoked the appointment on February 13, 1876. On April 5, Reed appointed A.D. Willey Under-Sheriff, revoked it on December 7, and appointed E.F. Henderson to the same position the same day.

By then 41-year-old James Reed was at the end of the term as sheriff. L.K. Myers replaced him in January 1877. Henderson served as Myers' under-sheriff for most of Myers' first year, resigning on November 13, 1877.[7]

◊

"Joe Thralls again did his job."

In 1876 Constable Joe Thralls found himself in the middle of another manhunt. The crime that precipitated this hunt dated back to the 1873 killing of William McDowell.

On the night of July 20, 1873, Texan Willis Jackson killed McDowell a few miles southwest of Wellington. Jackson scurried back to Texas to escape the consequences. He seemed to leave no tracks to his location.

By now most people involved with McDowell had left the scene. There was little doubt in anyone's mind as to Jackson being the killer. Jackson along with cattlemen H.G. Williams and J.J. Elkins, who were all involved in the crime, were no longer present to be arrested or even questioned. The town buzzed about the murder. No one seemed to know what to do. And nothing was done for two years.

Around that time Joe Thralls got involved. He never forgot the murder since it was committed while he was constable. He had thought about it since then and researched the possible places Jackson could be living.

On September 4th, 1875, Thralls mounted up and rode south, telling no one where he was headed or why. He arrived in Austin, Texas on September 24th. There he "produced a requisition" from Kansas Governor Thomas A. Osborne to Texas Governor Richard Coke which resulted in a warrant for Willis Jackson's arrest.

Thralls then headed for Wilson County, Texas, south of Austin, where he believed he would find Jackson. On the way there, he had to go through Seguin, Texas. In that town he got lucky. He spotted Jackson standing in the street.

As calmly as he could Thralls pulled out his gun, walked up to Jackson, and forced him to surrender. Thralls handcuffed him, put him on Thralls' horse, got on the horse himself and rode out of town headed back to Kansas. Thralls and his prisoner arrived in Wellington on October 9th.

Willis Jackson remained in the Wellington jail for the next six months waiting for his trial to take place. His lawyers, Blodgett and

83

Tucker, marshaled all the evidence they could to defend him. But there was too much evidence for the defense lawyers to overcome.

On April 26, 1876, Jackson was found guilty of first-degree murder. His lawyers tried to delay the sentence by making "a motion in arrest of judgment." District Judge W.P. Campbell scheduled a hearing on May 5th, and on that day overruled their motion. The judge then ordered Sheriff James Reed to bring the prisoners to court the next morning for final sentencing.

Jail guards stayed on duty that night to watch Jackson and several other prisoners. The prisoners were confined in an upstairs room. Several years later Jackson told what happened that night.

"I got out of [Wellington] without a cent of money or a single friend," he said. "There were six of them guarding us there. We had been playing cards in the back room. I got up and went into the other room to get some bedclothes to go to bed. As I came back I took a run for the window, put my hands on the sill and jumped out. I lit on the shanty roof below. It shook me up considerably but I went on and jumped to the ground.

"There was a big storm coming up and as soon as I got 40 feet away I knew all the men in Wellington couldn't catch me. When I got west of town, I got a horse and I felt safe then because no man in this country can ride with me.

"I got bewildered in the storm and took breakfast next morning with Ab Shearman's father-in-law (W.J. DeArmond) two miles north of town. I had my handcuffs on, but I made him believe I had a pistol. I asked him the road to Wichita, got my bearings, and struck northwest.

"At the head of the Medicine River I met five desperadoes and they took my handcuffs off. I rode the horse about 800 miles, then turned him loose and let him [go] home."[8]

How much truth there was in Jackson's own account of his escape could never be verified. But at least the part about him jumping out the window and disappearing in the night could. The guards watched it happen.

Joe Thralls couldn't help but feel bitterly disappointed with this outcome. He had done his job. And Jackson had been convicted. But all that seemed to be for nothing.

Thralls' bitterness turned to dogged determination. He decided he would track down Jackson again no matter how long it took. That stayed on his mind as he continued to serve as Wellington township constable.

◊

On Wednesday, August 2, 1876, at 4:10 p.m., Jack McCall shot and killed Wild Bill Hickok in Saloon No. 10 at Deadwood, Dakota Territory. Hickok had let down his guard by sitting at a table with his back to the room.

◊

By January 1877 the *Sumner County Press* showed John A. Kirk as Wellington city marshal, L.D. Wood and S.B. Rainy as constables, and James E. Reed as sheriff.[9] According to historian Richard L. Lane, Thralls had become a deputy U.S. marshal early in his career. It may have dated back to 1874 when he chased the Sumner County horse thieves.[10]

Though Thralls held no local position as a lawman for a while, he did work as a detective. He used his position as deputy U.S. marshal for legal authority to arrest fugitives when he had to. And he continued to think long and hard about how to catch Willis Jackson.

◊

That winter (1876-77) Joe Thralls was called on to find another killer. This kept him busy through most of 1877. And this time Thralls used more of his detective skills.

85

Some 170 miles east of Wellington at Pawnee, a town about 11 miles southwest of Fort Scott, a man named William Smith shot and killed Zack Potter on November 6, 1875. Smith escaped the scene and disappeared from sight.

The Bourbon county sheriff issued a warrant for Smith's arrest. But that was as far as the case got for more than a year. That's when Joe Thralls entered the picture.

Though the law lost track of Smith, people around Fort Scott didn't forget about the crime. Citizens there, including friends of the slain man, held out hope for justice.

But by the next winter, their hope was running out. After a year with no trace of the killer there was not much hope left. For some reason, perhaps because of his already growing reputation, Thralls was asked to track down the fugitive.

Thralls began his search for the fugitive by contacting other lawmen he knew. That included county sheriffs and deputy marshals throughout southern and eastern Kansas as well as Missouri and further. Since he'd worked as a constable and was now a deputy U.S. marshal, Thralls had developed a wide range of contacts. He had learned that the best way to catch a fugitive was to gather all available information before riding off. That way he could avoid the proverbial wild goose chase.

His correspondence with other lawmen soon paid off. He received a lead putting William Smith somewhere in Kentucky. Thralls headed that direction determined to find his man. In Kentucky he continued to correspond with lawmen. At first he couldn't pinpoint Smith's location. But Thralls had learned to be patient.

Back in Wellington, A.G. Vinson became city marshal and A.C. Vinson and E. Frank Henderson served as constables. L.K. Myers was sheriff.[11]

Thralls remained in Kentucky week after week looking for the right clue to lead him to the fugitive. Then one day the break came. By then Thralls had spent three months in the state, gathering information and waiting for the right opportunity. He received a tip on where Smith lived. And he quickly formed a plan. He would disguise himself and meet the fugitive face to face.

The day came and Thralls played his hand. Disguised, he casually walked up to Smith and struck up a conversation. At close range Thralls recognized Smith for who he was. But Smith had no idea who Thralls was. Still, Smith was wary of any strangers asking questions. And Thralls was a stranger. So Smith kept his guard up.

After the conversation, Thralls returned to his rented room and thought about his next step. At that late date he realized he lacked the proper official papers to arrest Smith.

Meanwhile Smith's nose for danger had forewarned him. His instincts had helped him escape the law before and it did so again. His conversation with Thralls told him there might be more to the man than he knew. So he quickly skipped out of the state, leaving no sign of his whereabouts. When Thralls learned that Smith was gone, he returned to Kansas empty handed, discouraged, but still determined.

Back in Kansas, Thralls gathered information from his sources. This time he received a lead from a Missouri deputy sheriff. The lawman told Thralls the fugitive Smith was in McMinn County, Tennessee.

Thralls wasted no time. He packed up and headed east to McMinn County, in southeastern Tennessee near the Appalachian Mountains. It was 900 miles distant. This time Thralls went better prepared. He carried a warrant for Smith's arrest.

After he arrived in Tennessee, Thralls gathered more information. He finally figured out where William Smith was staying. One of Thralls' connections spotted Smith at a nearby farmhouse. This time Thralls figured he had no time to double check the information. He quickly recruited a posse and headed to the farm.

A paper in Wellington reprinted an article from the *Fort Scott Daily Monitor* telling of Joe Thralls' experience. It described the outcome as follows.

"Upon arriving at the place [where Smith stayed], the house was surrounded. Smith, who was standing in front of the house, noticing their approach and circular movement, ran through one of the rooms out into the back yard where he was confronted by Mr. Thrall[s] with a drawn pistol.

"Smith stopped short, turned around and fled in an opposite direction into the hands of the posse, when he was secured. During this exciting event he was shot a number of times, several shots taking effect. But none of the wounds are considered dangerous. William Smith was now a prisoner of Mr. Thrall[s]."[12]

Joe Thralls headed back to Wellington relieved to have caught up with another criminal. But the Jackson case continued to frustrate him.

In January 1878, Thralls replaced A.G. Vinson as Wellington city marshal. A.G. Vinson, now known as the "smiling deputy sheriff," became a constable along with E. Frank Henderson. L.K. Myers was still sheriff.[13]

◊

With the Jackson case haunting him, Joe Thralls took on the task of trailing another killer. Now serving as Wellington city marshal and holding the position of a deputy U.S. marshal, Thralls by this time seemed to be the only person others in the area trusted to successfully pursue such a difficult job. Again this involved a killer who had escaped justice and left a cold trail.

Circumstance surrounding this shooting dated back to early 1878. In involved a cowboy, a trail boss couple, and a love triangle.

In September 1878, Marshal Thralls took on the job of tracking down a cowboy named Charles Lee. The events leading to this killing that called for Thralls' help grew out of a trip to Texas and back, which started in the spring of 1878.

That spring George W. Bowyer, a farmer who lived nine miles southwest of Wellington, headed to Coles City, Texas to buy cattle and bring them back to sell. Bowyer was well liked and highly respected by settlers in the Wellington area.

D. Newton Caldwell, a Wellington town leader then serving as city attorney, had been a close friend with Bowyer since childhood. They had grown up together in Illinois before coming west. Caldwell had served as Wellington's first mayor. He and Bowyer had continued to be close friends throughout their lives.

Mr. and Mrs. Bowyer had taken a hired hand, cowboy Charles Lee, and Mrs. Bowyer's sister, Mrs. Ceis, with them when they headed to Texas that spring of 1878. Lee, from Texas, had worked as a herder for Bowyer for about a year. Mrs. Ceis said she wanted to go along with them for her health. She left her young daughter at home with her husband.

On the way to Coles City, the Bowyers began to suspect something was going on between Mrs. Bowyer's sister Mrs. Ceis and Charles Lee. The Bowyers soon confirmed their suspicions. The party arrived at Coles City without incident. George Bowyer bought 350 head of cattle. Then they turned around and headed north back to Kansas.

On the way back, George told Mrs. Ceis he knew what was going on between her and Lee. George also notified Mr. Ceis back in Wellington of what he suspected. Mrs. Bowyer also told her sister she knew what was going. She even vented her feelings and told Lee to his face what she knew. This angered Lee. The further they traveled, the more incensed he became.

At one point Charles Lee threatened to kill George Bowyer. The Bowyers now feared for their lives. George tried several times to catch Lee without his gun strapped on. He had no success.

The further they traveled north, the worse it got. Often Lee would spend several hours in camp in the morning with Mrs. Ceis, forcing the Bowyers to herd the cattle by themselves. This crisis continued till they neared Indian Territory.

When they were about three miles south of Red River (about 15 miles northeast of Wichita Falls, Texas), the party reached a showdown. It took place Friday, August 16, 1878.

Bowyer asked Lee to give him his gun. The reason, Bowyer said, was because he knew Lee had threatened to kill him. Another reason was because Bowyer wouldn't tolerate Lee's behavior toward Mrs. Ceis. Bowyer refused to allow the lovers' tryst to continue.

Lee refused to give up his gun. Bowyer boiled in anger. "Get out of here and don't come back," he told the Texas cowboy. The Wellington paper described what followed.

"Lee at once approached his horse and taking a revolver from his holsters stepped behind the animal... Mrs. Bowyer warned her husband who was sitting on the ground with his back to Lee and at the same instant covered her husband's body with her own. Bowyer sprang to his feet and drew his pistol as Lee advanced. Both parties fired simultaneously."[14]

Lee's bullet hit Bowyer below his left ear, killing him instantly. He fell in the arms of his wife. Charles Lee then walked up to the couple, pushed Mrs. Bowyer away, and shot George twice more in the head and once in the chest.

The Bowyer party was at a well-traveled place with nearby farms when this happened. Others who heard the shots came to the scene. They helped Mrs. Bowyer bury the body. They also helped watch the cattle while Mrs. Bowyer returned to Cambridge, Clay County, Texas, a few miles south.

Mrs. Bowyer sent a telegram to Wellington addressed to W.S. Jones, who was her brother, Wesley. In it she told what had happened and asked for help in herding the cattle back to her home.

Back in Wellington the telegram arrived at the post office on Saturday, August 17. But no one claimed it. The first news about Bowyer's death came from a reporter in Cambridge, Texas who sent the news to the *Leavenworth Times* shortly after the fact. This news reached Wellington before the telegram was opened.

Once the news about Bowyer's death spread, the post office told Wesley Jones to pick up the message they were holding. The post office official suspected it contained the news the town had just heard from newspaper reports. Once Jones read the message, he told the authorities.

Town leaders asked Wellington City Marshal Joe Thralls, as a deputy U.S. marshal with outstanding credentials, to find Mrs. Bowyer and her cattle. Wellington City Attorney D. Newton Caldwell no doubt took part in the decision to have Thralls find Mrs. Bowyer.

Wellington citizens figured no one had more experience at this than Thralls, so he would have the best chance at success. Joe organized a group of men to accompany him and headed south.

Meanwhile back in Indian Territory, when Mrs. Bowyer sent her message she returned to the cattle. There she learned Charles Lee had decided to stay with the herd. Mrs. Bowyer had no choice but to follow. Lee, Mrs. Ceis, and Mrs. Bowyer traveled north together till they reached Pond Creek. There Lee changed his mind and decided to leave the herd. He and Mrs. Ceis continued north to Kansas on horseback, leaving Mrs. Boyer alone with the cattle.

Mrs. Bowyer knew she couldn't drive the cattle by herself. She decided to take the stage from Pond Creek to Kansas. She kept hoping someone would come with help, but she couldn't be sure. She was still in Indian Territory, where the worst outlaws roamed freely.

As her stagecoach approached Skeleton Creek, she noticed two horseback riders passing by. She recognized the riders. They were Charles Lee and her sister, who were still headed back to Kansas. Shortly after that, about 10 miles south of Caldwell, she recognized a group of horseman headed south. They were Joe Thralls and his men.

The Thralls party stopped in their tracks and returned to Kansas with Mrs. Bowyer. They took a break for food and rest at Caldwell. It was now Sunday, September 1.

While Mrs. Bowyer, Joe Thralls, and the posse were resting in Caldwell during lunchtime, Charles Lee and Mrs. Ceis rode up. They joined the Thralls group. Lee acted like he had done nothing wrong.

After everyone had rested, they decided to ride together on to William Jones farm nine miles southwest of Wellington. When they got to the Jones farm, William Jones' daughters (Mrs. Bowyer and Mrs. Ceis) along with Charles Lee, went inside.

At this time there must have been some doubt about who was to blame for the killing. At least Charles Lee acted that way. Otherwise he would not have relaxed there. He believed he could convince others that he was innocent of any crime.

Lee was mistaken. Others in Wellington who heard about the killing had little doubt about what had happened or who was guilty. Besides that, town leader D.N. Caldwell had no doubts about Lee's guilt and no reservations about telling others.

As Sunday evening approached, an observant person couldn't help but notice a gathering crowd of vigilantes ready to take Charles Lee by force. William Jones certainly got the message loud and clear. And for some reason he felt he needed to defend Lee. He told Lee to get out of the area if he valued his life. Lee finally caught on to his predicament. Quickly he rode off, leaving no evidence of where he was headed.

Monday morning, September 2, U.S. Commissioner J.P. Jones in Wellington issued a warrant for Charles Lee's arrest and handed it to Joe Thralls. But the warrant had come too late for Thralls to capture Lee at the Jones house. Thralls wouldn't consider giving up. He figured he had gained enough experience by then to do the job. And he was determined to bring Charles Lee to justice. He would spare no effort.

"Then commenced one of the most prolonged and remarkable manhunts in the history of the frontier," said Tom McNeal, an editor who later interviewed Thralls. According to McNeal, the man Thralls went after, Charles Lee, was extremely dangerous. He had already served at least one term in a Texas penitentiary.

"For nine months the big, quiet young frontiersman kept on the trail of the murderer," McNeal said. "He traced him through the Flint hills and nearly captured him in the neighborhood of Independence, but Lee managed to slip out of the trap and into the hills of southern Missouri. Thralls chased him out of there, back into Kansas [and] across the plains into Colorado. [He chased him] through the mountains and desert lands down into New Mexico [and] across the border into old Mexico. Back the fugitive turned and again crossed the border, this time into Texas, with Thralls still following with dogged persistence."[15]

Thralls lost track of Lee several times during this search. Each time, though, he would again pick up the trail. After several months of this tracking, Deputy U.S. Marshal Joe Thralls found Lee's trail leading into the Texas panhandle. This was a favorite hiding place for desperadoes on the run.

Thralls was several hundred miles away when he received information of Lee's whereabouts. Thralls knew the danger he faced in that area where fugitives found havens in scattered cattle camps. But he didn't feel he had a choice. So he kept on, single-minded in purpose. Through desolate land, sometimes mountainous, sometimes heated desert, Thralls continued in search of the Texas cowboy.

On June 16, 1879 the 30-year-old deputy marshal knew he was close.[16] He pinpointed a cattle camp where someone had spotted Charles Lee. It now had been 10 months since Thralls had begun his journey. Tom McNeal described what happened next.

"The big deputy marshal walked into a cow camp near the Panhandle border, covered Lee with his gun, quietly told him he was his prisoner, put the irons upon him, and started back on the long ride to Sumner County, Kansas."[17]

Charles Lee was sent to Fort Smith, Arkansas to be tried by "Hanging Judge" Isaac Parker. D.N. Caldwell assisted in the prosecution of Lee before the U.S. District Court there.[18]

Lee got lucky, especially in light of who Parker was. The hanging judge was not known for leniency and Lee was charged with murder. Lee got off with a 10-year sentence in the penitentiary for second-degree murder. According to McNeal, he served three or four years before he was pardoned and released.

But Joe Thralls had done his job. Again he was forced to spend a long period of time away from Wellington.

Local citizens welcomed him back. He soon became more popular and respected than ever. People looked to him as the epitome of an honest lawman who persistently pursued fugitives till they were captured.

◊

With an election less than five months away, 31-year-old Joe Thralls was persuaded to run as the Republican candidate for Sumner County sheriff. He had served as sheriff for that brief moment three years ago. But this time he hoped to hold on to that position a little longer.

8

"Sheriff Thralls is entitled to much credit."

Republicans welcomed Joe Thralls as a candidate for Sumner County sheriff. The Republican primary election confirmed their attitude. In September the local paper reported the results.

"The nominee for Sheriff, Mr. J.M. Thralls, of this city, was nominated on the first ballot, receiving more than a two thirds vote, or more than two to one over all his competitors."[1]

The paper, being run by Republicans, could be expected to favor Thralls over his Democrat opponent. But Editor John Folks' reasons for supporting Thralls still seemed strong. In the same issue he explained.

"Several of [Thralls'] successful efforts to capture and bring to punishment criminals after they had baffled or escaped from the authorities, are matters of record... He is of irreproachable character, temperate, and of the strictest business integrity."

Wellington citizens also believed in Joe Thralls' integrity. The ads more of less summarized what people already thought about him. Shortly before the election, The *Sumner County Press* ran the following:

"Since the beginning of the campaign, the Republican candidate for Sheriff has steadily grown in popular favor. During all these weeks not a word has been breathed against his capacity or integrity; while even those of diverse political faith, universally

95

admit that he possesses peculiar qualifications for the position, and hence ought to be elected, as he will be by a rousing majority.

"Personally, Mr. Thralls is without reproach. He is honest, capable, strictly temperate and every way worthy the support of the people of all classes and parties. Nature has indeed qualified him for the position for which he is a candidate. And adding to his natural abilities, his several years experience in the Detective Service, it may be readily seen that the estimation in which he is held by his friends is well based. His reputation and character as a citizen and official is unspotted; and every citizen desiring a capable and efficient administrator of the affairs of the Sheriff's office need not hesitate to cast his vote for J.M. Thralls."[2]

Yes, this was political rhetoric. But it reflected what people thought. Thralls sailed to an easy victory.

There may have been other candidates who could make similar claims, but Thralls had proved the claims. He had repeatedly shown a tenacious and uncanny ability to hunt down criminals. And he had shown a clean-cut character beyond reproach. It left little for his political opponents to work on.

No one was surprised when he won the election in November 1879. The figures revealed a lopsided victory. Totals showed 1,644 votes for Thralls; 984 for L.K. Myers, the Democrat, and 320 for J.F. Justus. That meant Thralls came close to beating his nearest opponent nearly two to one.[3]

The First Year

People who looked to Thralls for leadership in law enforcement expected much. Thralls did what he could to keep from disappointing them.

As Joe Thralls began his first term as sheriff, the Wellington city government went through some changes. The morning of January 19, 1880, the city council met in a special session. It discharged the city attorney, marshal, street commissioner, and policeman. That evening it appointed Thomas George as city attorney, C.C. Shawver as marshal (replacing R.W. Stevenson), and John Murphy as street commissioner. The city council didn't like the way the previous office holders enforced the law. Three months later, on April 9, the council appointed T.C. Gatliff, Jr. as marshal and B.A. Ellsworth as a policeman.[4]

On February 20, 1880 Governor John P. St. John proclaimed Wellington to be a city of the second class. On March 27 the Southern Kansas and Western Railroad was completed to Wellington. It was a branch of the Kansas City, Lawrence, and Southern Kansas Railroad. Another branch, the Sumner County Railroad, was built from Wellington to Hunnewell later that year. Besides these, The Cowley, Sumner, and Fort Smith Railroad, a branch of the Atchison, Topeka, & Santa Fe, was completed to Caldwell on June 13, 1880. This was barely in time for Texas cattlemen to trail their herds to Caldwell and Hunnewell for shipment east.

Once Joe became sheriff, he appointed Frank Evans as Under-Sheriff. Joe's brother Elzy became the jailor. The 1880 U.S. Census conducted in June listed six prisoners in the county jail. They included John W. Griffith, 32, a lawyer; Ed Clisbee, 31, a druggist; J.S. Bernard, 50, a farmer; Samuel Gilleland, 34, a "loafer;" W.R. Turner, 55, a physician; and Edgar Stout, 20, a herder (cowboy).[5]

These prisoners represented professional and businessmen more than farmers or ranchers. Lawyer John W. Griffith in fact had served as the Wellington city treasurer in 1879.

The Census showed that Joe Thralls and his brother Elzy roomed in the same house with a local implement dealer named C.E. Trowbridge. Others in the house included Trowbridge's wife, Louise; children Harry, 16 and Eddie, 15; Laura Day, 20, a "day servant," and Joseph P. Black, 20, Trowbridge's brother-in-law who worked as an implement dealer at his store.[6]

In his first year as sheriff, Thralls remained determined to catch convicted killer Willis Jackson. Citizens by 1880 had pretty well put Jackson out of their minds. But Joe Thralls hadn't. He definitely took his job as sheriff seriously and he saw, among other things, as a better opportunity to bring justice to the fugitive.

Caldwell

Joe began his job as Sumner County sheriff at the very time Caldwell entered its heyday. It would be a bloody time, especially for those who pinned on a badge. Though Thralls didn't anticipate Caldwell's bloodshed, he had enough experience under his belt to face it effectively.

Caldwell was founded in response to cattle drives. Wichita speculators saw an opportunity and took it. When Joseph McCoy drew cattlemen to Abilene in 1867, he directed them by way of the Chisholm Trail. Trail drivers had to go through Indian Territory before entering Kansas. If they made it through that area, they knew they had passed the greatest danger they would face on their trip.

Since Indian Territory remained hostile to cattlemen and had government restrictions such as prohibition to prevent traders from exploiting Indians, cowboys breathed a sigh of relief once they left the territory and entered Kansas. Wichita businessmen figured any business established along the trail in Kansas would be a cinch for success. In fact the first place inside Kansas (where Caldwell would be located) would be ideal because that's where cattlemen would stop for a drink. They couldn't do that in Indian Territory. That's why Wichita businessmen set their eyes on Caldwell.

But after it was established in 1871 the cattle business gradually shifted west for several reasons. Quarantine laws to keep tick-infected Texas longhorns from killing off local farmers' cattle gradually became more restrictive. And increasing numbers of settlers left decreasing room for cowboys to drive cattle through without interference.

By the middle 1870s most of the cattle traffic shifted west and headed for Dodge City. It looked like Caldwell would die out if something didn't change.

Caldwell had never been a final stop for cattlemen. It was simply the first place inside Kansas a cowboy could stop for a drink before continuing north. But Caldwell wanted their cattle trade also. With the cattle being diverted further west, Caldwell town leaders saw only one hope left for attracting the herds. If they could get a railroad to run through town, cattlemen could drive their herds to Caldwell and ship their live stock from there to the east by rail.

If this happened, Caldwell would have one key advantage over other cattle towns. It was so close to the border cattlemen could graze their stock in Indian Territory before shipping them east. That way the herders wouldn't have to deal with quarantine laws.

Caldwell leaders worked on several schemes trying to bring the railroad to town. And a number of them failed. Often the railroad company would ask for more money than people could raise. More often the railroads just didn't think a rail to Caldwell would make money.

But this changed in the late 1870s. Caldwell persuaded the Atchison, Topeka, and Santa Fe Railroad to build a branch through Sumner County all the way to their town. It would go from Mulvane through Belle Plaine and Wellington before reaching Caldwell. Originally called the Cowley, Sumner, and Fort Smith Railroad, it was completed in June 1880 (as previously mentioned).

Caldwellites were delighted. Business increased. It would have boomed beyond their imagination if it hadn't been for a competing railroad.

The Kansas City, Lawrence, and Southern Kansas Railroad decided to build a rail straight south of Wellington to Hunnewell, another border town. This also was completed in 1880 and was called the Sumner County Railroad.

Soon both Caldwell and Hunnewell were booming. Cowboys and cattlemen filled the saloons and purchased freely. As expected, this also brought more lawlessness and violence. Sheriff Thralls would have his hands full for the next two years.

The previous summer (1879) Caldwell was incorporated as a third class city. This meant it would have its first mayor, city council, and marshal.

It didn't take long for trouble to come to the Sumner County border cow town after that. While Caldwell had gone through some wild times in its early days, it had settled down during the late 1870s since fewer cattlemen went through the town.

As Dodge City received an increasing share of the cattle in the late 1870s, it experienced increasing violence and crime from the business. By 1878 it saw a number of shootouts and murders. To the careful observer, that suggested what was about to happen in Caldwell and Hunnewell for the same reason.

One other element added to Caldwell's problems. Increasing numbers of settlers gathered there as a jump off point for heading into Indian Territory to settle. Led by David Payne, they hoped to establish homesteads there and have the U.S. government approve of it later. These land "boomers" stirred up others in Caldwell.

"To this medley of humanity in Caldwell flocked the disreputables and criminal parasites that had been run out of Dodge City and Wichita by Wyatt Earp's sawed-off shotgun and Bat Masterson's flaming six-shooters," said Glenn Shirley. "Robberies and killings became so frequent that decent citizens were afraid to appear on the streets at night. Law enforcement consisted of preventing only the more heinous offenses, and it became a sacrifice of human life for officials to name a man to preserve order."[7]

Gunplay

A sign of what was to come in Caldwell took place in July 1879. Joe Thralls had just returned from catching murder suspect Charles Lee. What he heard about the Sumner County border town gave him an idea what he had to face if he became sheriff.

On Monday, July 7, 1879, some cowboys stirred up trouble near the Occidental Saloon in Caldwell. About 6 p.m. cowboys George Wood and Jack Adams arrived in Caldwell from Indian Territory. They along with Johnny Nicholson had just helped drive a herd of cattle to Caldwell from the Chickasaw Nation.

Wood and Adams, typical of cowboys, headed to the saloon for refreshments. Next they went outside where a band was playing and according the Wellington paper "began firing at blazing turpentine balls which some boys were tossing into the air." The Caldwell paper said the two cowboys were "egged on by one H.F. Harris, a sneak-thief ruffian."

Citizens complained. Wood and Adams returned to the Occidental Saloon for more drinks. Soon lawmen arrived outside the Occidental. Among them were Constable W.C.B. Kelly, Deputy Constable John Wilson and eight or nine posse members, including George W. Flatt.

The lawmen waited outside the saloon for a while hoping Wood and Adams would came back out soon. Some became impatient. Wilson and Flatt decided to go inside the saloon. Wilson walked to the back of the room in the saloon. Flatt followed but stopped at the bar in the front. Wood and Adams were near the bar drinking. The Wellington paper said Flatt laid his six shooters on the bar, called for a drink, finished it, then picked up his six shooters. The Caldwell paper said Wood and Adams cocked their guns. The Wellington paper said they "made a menacing movement toward Flatt."

At this point the Wellington paper and the Caldwell paper diverged in their accounts. The Wellington paper described what happened as follows:

"[Flatt] backed toward the door only two or three paces... Reaching the door first, Flatt stepped to the sidewalk and to the south side of the door. Wood and Adams... reached the door and [Adams] sprang to the sidewalk when the firing began. Adams received a fatal wound... Wood received two desperate wounds and staggered toward the inner door where he met Wilson who fired on

101

him. Wood fell to the floor. . . Wilson upon leaving the saloon was fired on by [W.H.] Kiser, one of the constable's posse, and slightly wounded. . ."

The Caldwell paper said Wood and Adams, after cocking their guns, headed for the front door. Flatt then backed toward the front door ahead of them. Then the guns came into play.

"On reaching the door, [Wood and Adams] leveled their six shooters on [Flatt] demanding his arms. Flatt replied, 'I'll die first.' And at that instant one of the fellows fired, the ball passing close by Flatt's head and grazed the temple of W.H. Kiser... Flat then drew both his pistols which he had kept concealed behind him and fired with the one in his right hand at the man who had got farthest out the door [Adams]... which caused [Adams] to drop heavily to the sidewalk and rolling off in the street died almost instantly.

"The man who stood in the door and shot first [Wood] received a ball in the right side which passed straight through his body from the pistol held in Flatt's left hand. The man returned the fire at Flatt, and then turned and fired at Wilson, who was closing in the rear. The ball grazed Wilson's wrist... Wilson returned the fire so rapidly that the man failed to get his work in... Wilson's first shot took effect in the right hand ... and the second in the abdomen ... from which [Wood] fell, shooting Wilson in the thigh as he went down."[8]

The two versions reflected two inquests. The first one was conducted by Coroner James M. Thomas and a jury of six people shortly after the incident and continued into the next morning. The second was conducted by Sumner County Coroner John H. Folks two days after the incident. Though the two versions disagreed as to whether Wood and Adams fired any shots, both versions agreed that lawmen were justified in what they did. This was the beginning of a number of shootings in Caldwell.

The day before the shooting, Joe Thralls headed for Topeka, Kansas. He had with him Charles Lee, the man who shot and killed George Bowyer in 1878. Thralls had caught him on June 16, 1879 in the Texas panhandle and was sending Lee on the first leg of his journey to Fort Smith, Arkansas, to stand trial.

Thralls had no illusions about the job he faced in his first year as sheriff. The Caldwell killings had happened before Thralls even ran for office. He knew such things most likely would continue to occur as he served out his term as head lawman.

People in Caldwell saw George Flatt as a hero. Wellington citizens put him on a lower plane.

Flatt soon took advantage of the hero worship he received and went into business. He took on a partner, William Horseman, and opened a saloon located near the City Hotel in Caldwell. Two weeks after the Caldwell shootout the town incorporated. A month later the Caldwell paper published a new ordinance detailing the duties and pay for a city marshal. The salary came to $400 a year to be paid monthly.

The new mayor, Noah J. Dixon, and city council had no doubt about their leading candidate. They chose George Flatt. In the last few weeks Flatt had been elevated to the position of a deadly and fearless gunfighter willing to risk his life to protect citizens.

He soon began making arrests, the first being J.H. Wendels, charged with driving too fast. In October Flatt and his deputy, Dan Jones, got into their first shooting spree. Jones, as mentioned earlier, served as a constable in Wellington back in the early 1870s with Joe Thralls. He had moved to Red Fork Ranch in Indian Territory, but some time after that moved to Caldwell.

The only shooting incident recorded during Marshal Flatt's term happened on October 29, 1879. That afternoon Flatt and Jones tried to arrest a cowboy named John Dean for carrying firearms in town, which was against a new ordinance. The cowboy got on his horse, fired his pistol, then began riding out of town. Flatt and Jones ran after him on foot yelling for him to stop. Dean turned around and shot at them. Flatt and Jones opened fire but no rounds found their target. Deputy Jones filed a complaint and Dean was arrested. He pled guilty and was fined.

A Lawman for Breakfast

George Flatt served as Caldwell's marshal till the city election on April 5, 1880. Mike Meagher, former marshal of Wichita who became the next Caldwell mayor, then appointed William Horseman to replace Flatt.

Flat stayed in town and continued in law as a detective. But his popularity shrunk as his drinking habit grew. Other lawmen in Caldwell resented his arrogance and belligerence. He often threatened or made fun of the police force.

Little more than two months later, at about one a.m. Saturday morning, June 19, 1880, Flatt's role in Caldwell ended. That Friday evening the 27-year-old recently married former marshal met his destiny. Who was behind what happened that day remains a mystery.

On the previous evening, Thursday, June 17, Flatt pulled a gun on Marshal William Horseman and threatened to shoot his feet off. He also threatened Policeman Frank Hunt. At least that's what Horseman said.

The following evening, Friday, June 18, Flatt frequented several saloons. The later it got, the drunker Flatt got. By midnight Flatt had gone from the Red Light dance hall to the Kentucky Saloon to the I.X.T. Saloon, where he often slept in the back room.

Samuel H. Rogers, a city policeman, was with him and feared for his safety. Rogers knew the way others on the police force felt about him. They feared Flatt and hated him for making them look foolish.

Rogers tried to get Flatt to go home to his new wife. Next he tried to get him to sleep it off in the I.X.T. Flatt refused. "I want to go and take a lunch first," he told Rogers.

So Rogers stayed with Flatt as they headed to Louis Segerman's Restaurant. Another friend, Charles L. Spear went along. The three men walked south on Main Street from the I.X.T. toward Segerman's. Spear walked nearest the buildings to his left and slightly ahead of Flatt at his right. Rogers walked slightly behind and to the right of Flatt. It was around one a.m.

As the three men passed the bank building, H.A. Ross, the town jeweler heard Flatt say, "I'm the cock of the walk of Caldwell."

When the three men were about 100 feet from the northwest corner of Fifth and Main, a shotgun blast cut through the night air. Spear thought in came from behind them. Rogers said it deafened his left ear and sounded like it came from a little above him, perhaps from an awning. Flatt fell face forward, dead when he hit the ground.

Blasts from other guns came fast and furious, filling Flatt with additional lead. These came from across the street. Sam Rogers called out, "Let up, you've killed that man."

First ones on the scene after the gunshots were Mayor Mike Meagher, Marshal William Horseman, Constable/Assistant Marshal Dan Jones, and Policeman Frank Hunt. Soon Judge James D. Kelly, Sr. and Dr. William A. Noble arrived. Noble examined the body and pronounced Flatt dead. Several men carried the body to Peter B. Hohler's barbershop.

County Coroner John H. Folks arrived by train later that morning. He began an inquest. The inquest continued publicly through Monday. Starting on Tuesday morning, Folks held it in secret.[9]

Unwelcome Duty Calls

Three days later, Friday, June 25, Sheriff Joe Thralls with several of his deputies came to Caldwell by train with arrest warrants. He arrested Mayor Mike Meagher, Marshal William Horseman, Constable Dan Jones (who had worked with Thralls in Wellington), and Policemen Frank Hunt and James Johnson. Thralls also summoned Dan Rogers, Charles Spear, Hugh A. Ross, Dr. D. MacMillan, and William Thompson as prosecution witnesses.[10]

This arrest likely came hard for Thralls. He had known Dan Jones since their earliest days as constables in Wellington. As a lawman for the last eight years, Thralls probably knew all of the lawmen in Caldwell and hated to think of taking them in.

Who or what was behind these arrests has never come to light. It could have been the verdict of the secret inquest. It could have been that another secret witness came forward with information. Whatever it was, Wellington leaders believed the Caldwell police force murdered George Flatt.

The prisoners and witnesses from Caldwell left with Thralls on the 2:20 p.m. train to Wellington that day. Their trial began the following Monday and closed Wednesday evening, June 30.

That same day the Caldwell city council fired Horseman and his deputies. On July 3 Horseman, Hunt, Jones, and Johnson were bound over for the next session of district court and their bail set at $500 each.

On July 8 Caldwell rehired Horseman and his deputies. A week later Sheriff Thralls again arrested Horseman and Hunt, this time for assault and battery of Abram Rhodes. Horseman and Hunt were eventually released but the Caldwell city council again changed its mind. On August 10 it again fired Horseman and hired James Johnson. The *Caldwell Post* reported Horseman resigned.[11] The rest of the police force remained.

Joe Thralls felt like he was caught in the middle of a political battle rather than a criminal case. He had sworn to uphold the law and so he carried out his duties but not with much enthusiasm. He could see that Caldwell was becoming a thorn in his flesh.

Luckily Thralls heard no more major trouble from Caldwell for a couple of months. Even Caldwell thought it had finally settled down.

Professional Manhunt

In September 1880 Joe Thralls went after a notorious horse thief named Dave Sprague. Back on July 23rd, an Albany, Missouri lawman arrested Sprague at Burlingame, Kansas. But Sprague must have had influential friends. He was soon released "under suspicious circumstances."

Sheriff Thralls was acquainted with Sprague from past incidents. He knew Sprague's weaknesses. Sprague loved horse racing and often visited racetracks. So Thralls followed him from one place to another until he found the chance to close in. On Thursday, September 23, Sprague led Thralls to a Lawrence, Kansas fair. There Thralls arrested him.

Thralls notified Sheriff Allen from Osceola, Iowa, the place Sprague was wanted. Knowing Sprague to be slippery, Thralls went along with the other lawmen as they took Sprague on the first leg of the journey through northeast Kansas into Missouri.

Sprague had already filed one habeas corpus in Topeka and another in Lawrence hoping to escape legally. He claimed they had the wrong man and swore his name was J.K. Oliver. None of this did any good because Thralls already knew who he was. And now Thralls made sure Sprague left the state.

Iowa citizens were impressed with Thralls ability. "Sheriff Thralls is entitled to much credit from citizens of the county for sticking to Sprague till he caught him," said the Decatur, Iowa *Journal*.[12]

More Caldwell Trouble

Thralls didn't have long to wait before he heard of more trouble back in Caldwell. That's not what the town leaders wanted and it's not what they expected. In fact, on October 4, 1880 the town laid off all of its police force except for Marshal James W. Johnson. Town leaders felt so confident lawlessness was a thing of the past that they convinced citizens including newsmen of this.

For example, the *Caldwell Post* said, "The police court is terribly quiet. No arrests, no drunks, no nothing. If the police keep up this kind of racket, the calaboose will lose all its interest and only be fit for a chicken coop."[13]

Four days after the police force left, gunfire shattered the supposed peaceful town. On Friday, October 8, between 10 and 11 p.m., a gunman shot Frank Hunt, who had served as a policeman under William N. Horseman and James W. Johnson.

Hunt was sitting near a north window at the Red Light Saloon, located at Fifth and Chisholm, when someone from outside fired through the open window. The bullet hit Hunt in the left side, went through his liver and lodged in the right side of his stomach. Hunt pointed to the window and called out, "I'm killed! He did it out there!"

Marshal James W. Johnson and special policeman Dan W. Jones, who were at the Red Light, ran for the east door. The east door was stuck, so Jones went out the front door. Johnson finally forced the east door open and ran to the north side of the building. He heard someone running away but could see nothing since the night was dark.

The shooter escaped. Several men carried the fatally wounded Hunt to the Leland Hotel. Monday morning Hunt died.

Judge James Kelly held an inquest. The inquest concluded that Hunt "came to his death from a pistol ball fired from a pistol held in the hand of David Spear . . . and that this was done feloniously and with malice aforethought, and . . . that one Lumis or Loomis, at that time engaged as night-watch at the Red Light Saloon ... was an accessory before the fact."[14]

Young David Spear (age 17) was quickly arrested. Loomis made his escape to Wellington, where Sheriff Thralls caught him. Spear was tried on October 22 and released. No records show what happened to Loomis.

Tracking Jackson

That week Joe Thralls returned to an unfinished job that had plagued him for the last several years. He slipped out of town nearly unnoticed and headed to Texas to haul back a prisoner. The prisoner was Texas killer Willis Jackson.

He was the man who had murdered William McDowell near Wellington back on July 21, 1873. Most people by 1880 had forgotten about that incident. Thralls hadn't.

Thralls had remained just as determined to catch Jackson in 1880 as he had been back in 1875. That was the year he caught the Texan. He hauled him to Wellington, saw Jackson convicted of first-degree murder on April 26, 1876, only to have him escape on May 6, the day he was to be sentenced. McDowell jumped out of the courthouse window and scurried off without a trace. Thralls' single-minded aim to again capture Jackson typified the lawman's character.

No doubt Thralls took special interest in Jackson. It may have been because of how easily Jackson escaped justice. It may have been because of Thralls' deeply ingrained sense of justice. It may have been a touch of wounded pride in knowing the outlaw had got the best of lawmen, though it hadn't been Thralls' fault. Whatever the reason, Thralls was now on his way to put an end to the outlaw's freedom.

Thralls had been working behind the scenes for some time. The previous June he had contacted lawmen in Texas about Willis Jackson. He described the man – six foot, lean, and light complexion, black hair and heavy mustache, gray eyes. Through contacts he found out Jackson was living in Wilson County, Texas.

He sent Texas lawmen a requisition to arrest the outlaw and waited for their reply. He didn't expect to wait five months, but he did. Eventually his groundwork got results. On October 20 Thralls received a notice from the Texas Rangers that Jackson had been caught. That's when he headed to Texas to pick up the outlaw.

On Thursday, October 28, Thralls returned to Wellington with his prisoner. He again put him in the county jail. Willis Jackson seemed to enjoy talking to newspaper reporters about his escape in 1876, bragging about how easy it was. But he refused to talk about the killing. Joe Thralls was just glad to have the outlaw behind bars.[15]

On November 29, Frank Evans resigned as Under-Sheriff. Joe then appointed his brother, Elzy, to replace Evans on December 2.

9

"His re-election is foreordained."

The year 1881 started out similar to the year before. A man named L.H. Fisher made charges against the marshal, T.C. Gatliff, Jr., and a policeman, Ben Ellsworth, accusing them of "various misdeeds." On January 12, the city council met to try the two lawmen. Gatliff resigned before the trial. Ellsworth didn't. The council found him guilty. Then he resigned.

The council appointed J.D. Forsyth as the new marshal. But the council wasn't through. On March 14 they dismissed the entire police force and appointed John I. Anderson as marshal. This was not the time to be a city lawman in Wellington.

Sheriff Thralls no longer found himself surprised by lawlessness in Caldwell. He could see the increasingly busy and crowded cow town as inevitably spawning violence. The most he could hope for was to keep it under relative control.

In March 1881 the sheriff helped out a fellow lawman named Cole. Detective Cole told Thralls about an outlaw who was then thought to be living in Caldwell. The man Cole referred to was accused of highway robbery. His name was James M. Moreland.

Moreland's crime dated to the previous year. At that time a young man named McGraw came from Michigan to Wichita, Kansas with $1,000 on him to purchase land. In Wichita, McGraw happened to meet a man named Count Roberts.

Roberts told McGraw about two friends, James Moreland and Dick Baker, who lived at Marion Center in Marion County, Kansas.

Roberts said that his two friends would be glad to help McGraw find the right land to buy. They would even provide a free team of horses so McGraw could check out the lay of the land.

So Roberts took McGraw to Marion Center where McGraw met Moreland and Baker. Soon after meeting, the three men tried to get McGraw to invest his money with them, but McGraw wouldn't.

Next, Roberts offered to go with McGraw in the wagon as the Michigan man scouted for land to buy. This sounded like a good idea to McGraw. The two men headed out.

When they'd ridden about 20 miles, they noticed two masked men headed their way. The men on horseback began firing. Roberts jumped out of the wagon.

The masked men held up McGraw and took his money as well as his watch and chain and other valuables. McGraw recognized the two men as James Moreland and Dick Baker, but at the time he was glad to escape with his life.

Stripped of all his valuables, McGraw left the place in search of a job. He ended up in Burlingame, Kansas working on a farm. There he told several others of his experience being robbed.

Moreland and Baker somehow found out McGraw had fingered them. They kidnapped him at gunpoint, took him to a magistrate, and forced him to sign an affidavit exonerating them.

Again, McGraw felt lucky to escape alive. He headed back to Michigan.

McGraw's friends, though, weren't ready to drop the matter. They hired Cole, a Topeka, Kansas detective, to get to the bottom of the case. That's when Cole tracked down the men and asked for help from Sheriff Thralls.

Roberts was captured in Wichita. Baker was found in New Mexico. And Joe Thralls caught James Moreland in Caldwell on Wednesday, March 16, 1881.[1]

◊

112

Later that month Sheriff Thralls made a trip to Camp Supply in Indian Territory. He returned on Monday, March 28, with a prisoner, Delos Nelson, believed to be a horse thief. By now, Thralls took this kind of work in stride.

Undesirable Duty

But sometimes Sheriff Thralls had to deal with cases not related to cowboys, horse thieves, or gunfights. At least one case involved an abortion.

On Thursday, April 28th, friends of Mrs. Amanda Thompson sent a telegram to Wellington. They insisted that the county conduct an inquest on her death. Mrs. Thompson lived on the second floor of a wing of the Oxford House in Oxford, Kansas.

Thompson had died suddenly on Wednesday night, April 27th. Coroner John H. Folks, Deputy County Attorney J.W. Haughey, and Sheriff Joe Thralls left the city and arrived in Oxford that evening. Mrs. Thompson had lived at this place with W.H. Richardson, the building owner, and Mrs. Clara J. Reed for more than a year.

The inquest began Thursday night. Dr. J.A. Maggard arrived later from Wellington and examined the body.

The inquest concluded on Saturday evening, April 30th. At that time the jury decided that, "Mrs. Amanda Thompson came to her death ... from the effects of Oil of Tansy, taken by, or administered to [her] by William H. Richardson and Mrs. Clara J. Reed ... with the intention of ... producing an abortion upon the person ... and that the said Oil of Tansy was procured and furnished by William H. Richardson with a knowledge of the purpose for which it was intended to be taken by or administered to the said deceased."

Sheriff Thralls received a warrant for the arrest of Richardson and Reed. This time Thralls had no desire to serve it. He gave it to his deputy, D.A. Hills, who made the arrest.

The Wellington paper editorialized that "in the light of the evidence accumulated and recorded, the jury was fully justified in returning the verdict that will place the accused parties on trial for complicity in the crime that resulted in the death of the unfortunate victim of a villain's unlawful lust."

The court never convicted the two. Richardson and Reed were discharged on May 6th.[2]

◊

On May 1st, the new Kansas Prohibition statute went into effect. On May 9, Freeman and Scott made the first shipment of cattle that season from Hunnewell. The two events clashed. Cowboys ignored the prohibition law.

Honing His Technique

Early in May Sheriff Thralls had letters printed up to notify people in the area about a horse thief. The thief had sold a stolen horse to the Hastie and Day livery stable in Wellington. Thralls by now regularly sent out circular letters to track down wanted men.

The letters went out on a northbound four p.m. train on Wednesday, April 11. The letters described Charles Tyrol, 19, from Dubuque, Iowa, and offered $50 reward for his capture. This was the standard county reward offered for fugitive criminals.

When a liveryman in Sedgwick City received a copy, he recognized Charles Tyrol as a man in the area. He telegraphed Thralls with the information. Joe left on the four p.m. train on Thursday. Andy A. Richards, who would become the new editor of the *Sumner County Press* on August 16, was also on the train. And he saw Thralls.

"I noticed our Sheriff J.M. Thralls, supplied as usual with a complete set of iron bracelets," he said. "A few inquiries developed the fact that he was bound for Sedgwick City to take in charge a horse thief which he had intercepted by a circular mailed the day previously."[3]

Thralls got off the train at Sedgwick City while Richards continued on to Dodge City, where he was greeted by a coronet band. Thralls captured and handcuffed Charles Tyrol. He left the next morning with his prisoner and arrived in Wellington at 11 a.m. He jailed him in time for lunch.

◊

On Thursday, July 14, Sheriff Pat Garrett shot and killed Henry McCarty (Billy the Kid) at Fort Sumner, New Mexico. That month Hunnewell shipped 525 carloads of cattle.

◊

On August 6, several Hunnewell dance hall customers feuded. Three died in the battle: William Gilchrist, Sr., William Gilchrist, Jr., and Alexander Gilchrist. Thralls cast a worried eye that direction, hoping more trouble wouldn't follow.

Andy Richards, like most Sumner County residents, then admired Thralls. This would change two years later. But in 1881, the new editor of the *Press* described Thralls in glowing terms.

"Long before elected to the office, J.M. Thralls did all the dangerous work connected with the enforcement of laws in Sumner County," he said. "He is the only man who ever brought a man back to Sumner County on a requisition [Willis Jackson]. His career as Sheriff has been a busy and brilliant one and without a stain to his honor. His re-election is foreordained."[4]

◊

On Thursday, August 18 there was more trouble in Caldwell. Charley Davis shot and killed George Woods, proprietor of the Red Light Saloon. The two men quarreled over Lizzie Roberts. She had lived with Davis before leaving him to live at the Red Light.

When Davis tried to get her to return to him, she protested and Woods took Roberts' side. Davis shot Woods from about a yard away. Davis was arrested but soon escaped and left town.[5] Joe Thralls took note of the incident but had little control over what happened in Caldwell while he was in Wellington. He was becoming more frustrated each time the Caldwell body count increased.

On Sunday, August 28, Sheriff Thralls arrested John T. Bennett somewhere between South Haven and Clear Dale. Nez Perce Indians had accused Bennett of stealing their cattle and Thralls believed them. In fact, Thralls seemed to have evidence that Bennett had been doing this for the last three years.

That afternoon a Mr. Hazzard visited Bennett at the jail. Thralls later found out Bennett tried to persuade Hazzard to obliterate the brand on the cattle Bennett had stolen. Thralls took Bennett to Fort Smith, Arkansas to be tried in Federal Court.[6]

◊

On Tuesday, September 13, the Republican county convention nominated Joe Thralls for re-election as sheriff. Editor Andy Richards promoted Sheriff Thralls in ever more glowing terms.

"J.M. Thralls, the candidate for re-election as Sheriff, is the man of all men for this position," he said. "His natural tact as a detective and his successful operations as an executive officer have given him an enviable reputation that knows no county or state boundaries. From the Mississippi to the Rockies, Joe Thralls is known and honored by all officers of the law and dreaded by all lawbreakers. Personally he is cool, temperate, rigidly honorable and of irreproachable character. His career as Sheriff is unblemished. His re-election will be supported by voters without respect to party and redound to the honor of our county."[7]

◊

Rowdy cowboys continued to plague Thralls' with their recklessness. This time it came from the new cow town south of Wellington.

Around noon on Tuesday, September 27, three cowboys in Hunnewell stirred up trouble. Albert Chastain, Bill Mills, and Allen Carter began firing their pistols in a dance house where they had been drinking all morning. When they walked out and jumped on their horses, they continued firing randomly as they rode through town. They headed toward the depot, sometimes riding on the sidewalk while firing into buildings along the way.

Most citizens ran for cover. The mayor, At Hughes, didn't. He leveled a double-barreled shotgun at the cowboys and opened fire. Chastain received a blast in his face. Mills took a hit in the small of his back. His horse was hit and killed. Carter and Chastain began firing into a crowd that had gathered on the sidewalk.

Sadie Colder, an 18-year-old who was standing nearly a block away, fell to the ground dead. One bullet had struck her in the right eye.

The three cowboys rode out of town on two horses, Mills riding behind Chastain. They headed for Indian Territory. But Mills couldn't go far. Chastain left him off near town and continued south. Hunnewell citizens quickly found Mills and hauled him back to town. He barely escaped hanging. They brought him to Wellington on a special train that night and put in jail.

About 30 men from Hunnewell chased the other two for 15 miles before catching them. This posse believed Chastain and Carter would never escape the hangman's rope if they went back to Hunnewell, so they took the two prisoners straight to Wellington where they were put in jail.[8]

This incident confirmed Sheriff Thralls' greatest worries about his job. Hunnewell along with Caldwell were definitely the places to watch in the future. Thralls had his work cut out for him, especially if he continued as sheriff for a second term.

◊

Both Caldwell and Hunnewell had the potential to end up in a gunfight like the one that took place a month later further west. On Wednesday, October 26, in Tombstone, Arizona, Wyatt Earp and party shot and killed three cowboys near the OK Corral. What would be Joe Thralls' Tombstone?

10

A Great Reputation Captured

As the county elections drew near, few people, including Democrats, doubted Joe Thralls would be re-elected. Editor Andy A. Richards said, "Joe M. Thralls has an easy road to Sheriff. True, Joseph Sleigh, of Oxford, and J.P. Elsie, of Green Township, are candidates, but they are not dangerous. Mr. Thralls' record in Sumner County will elect him by an overwhelming majority. Neither of his opponents consider it worthwhile to spend time or talents in the campaign."[1]

They were right. The county overwhelmingly re-elected Thralls in November 1881. He entered this term with much more experience in the job than the first term, but with lingering worries about the county.

Fire

Fire was a constant threat to early towns. With inadequate firefighting equipment and mostly wood buildings, a town could quickly go up in smoke.

About 2:30 a.m. on November 3, flames enveloped Wellington's business district, leaving a city block of businesses destroyed. Sheriff Thralls was at the jail when the fire broke out. Ever vigilant, he viewed the situation with typical caution.

"Joe Thralls saw the fire from the jail," said the *Press*, "and suspecting it might be a scheme to fire the town and then attack the jail and rescue the prisoners, or a part of them, he fired several shots that aroused all that end of town."[2]

Banker Trouble

Early in December, Joe Thralls nearly had another lynching on his hands. This time the culprit was not a horse thief or a murderer. He was a banker.

J.S. Danford, president of Merchants and Drovers Bank of Caldwell, ran into trouble in the last weeks of November. Rumors began to spread that his bank was on the brink of failure. People trusted Danford, who told them the bank had a temporary shortage of money but nothing else. They gave Danford the benefit of a doubt. In fact, some deposited more money in the bank they otherwise would have simply to help out with the "temporary shortage."

The problem was, while the bank took deposits into Saturday afternoon, December 3, the bank cashier, W.D.C. Smith, skipped town that same afternoon, taking securities with him. The early Sunday morning Smith met Danford in Wellington. There Danford deeded the bank building to Major Hood. Both men then left Wellington in a private carriage headed from Wichita early Sunday morning.

The word somehow got out about their flight and I.B. Gilmore in Wellington quickly swore out a warrant for their arrest. Sheriff Thralls then sent a telegram to Sedgwick County Sheriff H.R. Watt in Wichita. Watt arrested Danford and Smith. He telegraphed Sheriff Thralls to meet him at Mulvane and then headed south.

The prisoners were scheduled for a preliminary hearing before Judge Torrance in Winfield on Sunday evening. When Sedgwick County Sheriff Watt got to Mulvane, Thralls had not yet arrived though a party from Winfield had. Meanwhile Wellington had sent a telegraphed copy of the Danford and Smith arrest warrant to Mulvane.

When Sedgwick County Sheriff Watt saw the warrant in Mulvane, he headed to Wellington before the Caldwell posse arrived in Mulvane. Had the Caldwell posse arrived sooner in Mulvane, no telling what would have happened to Danford and Smith.

In Wellington, a number of creditors from Caldwell led by Constable Abram Rhodes, who were more like a lynch mob, were waiting to question Danford. They forced him to return to Caldwell. Danford was able to convince them to go by train after he offered to pay the fair. That afternoon nearly a hundred people from Caldwell with Danford arrived by train.

On Tuesday morning, creditors met and adopted a resolution holding Danford responsible for every penny he owed. The legal battle would continue for several years. Though Danford avoided a lynching, his health declined for a while. He would never forget how close he came to a hangman's rope.[3]

Talbot Raid

Later that month, Sheriff Thralls had to deal with more trouble in Caldwell. Cowboys and lawmen fought in the streets of the border town on Saturday, December 17, 1881.[4]

After the bullets stopped, two men were dead: Caldwell's former mayor Mike Meagher and Red Light Saloon and Dance Hall owner George Spear. James D. Sherman, alias Jim Talbot, led the cowboys in their shootout.

Talbot, along with his wife and two children, had arrived in Caldwell six or eight weeks before the shooting began. He had helped trail Texas cattle to Caldwell for a man named Millet. Talbot rented a house from lawman Dan W. Jones on the east side of town north of Fifth and Chisholm. Soon several other cowboys moved in with him. They included Bob Bigtree, Dick Eddleman, Doug Hill, Tom Love, Jim Martin, and Bob Munson.

After several weeks in Caldwell, these cowboys were becoming restless to return to Texas. Shortly before they planned to leave, they went to the opening night of the play, "Uncle Tom's Cabin," at Caldwell's opera house at the southeast corner of Fifth and Main. It was Friday, December 16.

Soon the cowboys created a disturbance, talking and cursing loudly while the play continued. Tell W. Walton, editor of the *Caldwell Post* who sat nearby, asked Talbot to quiet down. Talbot told Walton, "I'll fix you tomorrow."

After the play, the Talbot cowboys went from one saloon to another, drinking, carousing, and swearing to fix Mike Meagher and Editor Walton in the morning. Next morning the cowboys began shooting up the town.

Mike Meagher felt he had to stop the cowboys before worse things happened. That morning, December 17, he went to Marshal John Wilson's house and told him the danger. Wilson and Meagher then headed downtown.

From that time on during the day the situation got worse. Wilson and Meagher saw the cowboys still celebrating, armed with rifles and pistols. They then heard a gun blast inside Moore's Saloon. Wilson entered the saloon, found Tom Love to be the shooter, disarmed him, and headed him toward the jail.

The other cowboys began to surround Wilson as he walked with Tom Love. When Meagher tried to help, the cowboys knocked him down and threatened to kill him. Wilson told Meagher to run up the opera stairs while Wilson watched his back.

In this confusion, Tom Love escaped. The cowboys went to Comanche Bill Mankin's house (about a half block west of Talbot's) to figure out what to do next. For a few hours the streets remained quiet. But Marshal Wilson worried that he hadn't seen the last of the cowboys.

Around noon Wilson sent a telegram to Caldwell Mayor Cass Burrus telling him of the dangerous situation. Burrus was in

Wellington at the time. He had the noon train to Caldwell wait while he asked Sheriff Thralls to form a posse and go with him back to Caldwell. Mayor Burrus, Sheriff Thralls, and a 20-man posse arrived in Caldwell around 3 p.m.

In the meantime, trouble was brewing in Caldwell. Around one p.m., the cowboys started roaming around town again. Lawmen arrested Jim Martin for carrying a weapon and resisting arrest. They took him to the police judge, who fined him. Since Martin had no money on him, Deputy Marshal Will D. Fosset went with him to get some.

Martin never made it to the bank. Cowboys Talbot, Love, Munson, and Eddleman walked up to Marshal Fosset. Fosset drew his revolver. The cowboys ran for cover. As Jim Talbot sought cover, he fired several rounds. This happened just north of Fifth and Main. That started a gun battle between the cowboys and the town that left the area bullet riddled.

The cowboys ran east to Talbot's house for more weapons and ammunition. Talbot got another rifle there, then headed back west toward Main. When he reached the alley to the east of the opera house, he looked south and spotted Mike Meagher. Talbot opened up on Meagher, firing several rounds before one bullet tore through Meagher's body. "I'm hit, and hit hard." Meagher groaned. Marshal Wilson, who was nearby, left Meagher to chase Talbot.

Ed F. Rathbun, who was at the back of Pulaski's store, also saw Talbot shoot Meagher. "Good God, Mike, are you hit?" he gasped.

"Yes. Tell my wife I've got it at last."

Meagher still had a six-shooter in his right hand and a rifle under his left arm as Rathbun helped him get to the barbershop. He died a short time later.

The cowboys then headed north to George Kalbfleisch's livery stable on Fourth Street. They figured it was time to leave town. At the stable they forced Kalbfleisch to give them horses for their getaway. George Spear sympathized with the cowboys. As he helped saddle up a horse for them, he stopped a bullet, and fell dead.

All but two of the cowboys rode out of town on horseback. It was around 1:30 p.m. Dick Eddleman and Tom Love's luck ran out. They had no horses to ride. So they hid in the stable hoping somehow to escape later.

Mayor Burrus, Sheriff Thralls, and Thralls' 20-man posse arrived about an hour and a half after all the shooting. Thralls found Eddleman and Love in the stable and arrested them.

Earlier the incensed townsmen had followed close behind the fleeing cowboys. About a mile from town the cowboys met up with a farmer hauling an extra horse to town. They took it for themselves and continued south.

As they approached Deer Creek at the Deutcher ranch about 10 miles south of Caldwell, the cowboys could see townsmen close behind. The cowboys were desperate. Then they spotted a canyon. They also noticed a dugout in the canyon. They ran for cover just in time to hide from flying bullets.

Soon townsmen had the canyon surrounded. They figured the cowboys were trapped. The sun was setting. The cowboys and townsmen continued to exchange shots. But it soon became apparent the cowboys had the advantage. They could see their pursuers clearly on the ridge of the canyon while the townsmen had to put themselves in harm's way to view the cowboys who were hiding behind walls.

That didn't stop local rancher Wilbur Emery Campbell from trying to flush the cowboys out. He slid down an opening to the canyon for a closer view. Gunshots quickly filled the air, some hitting Campbell.

"I'm hit," he called to his companions. One bullet went through his wrist and another through his clothes. His companions helped him get away. He bled profusely. Several left with him headed for a doctor in Caldwell.[5]

As the sun set, only six townsmen remained to guard the canyon. Shortly after Campbell and others left, the cowboys escaped.

So Sheriff Thralls and his posse arrived at the scene too late to catch up with the desperadoes, though no one realized it at first.

The posse found this out in the morning. Once they did, most of the townsmen headed back to Caldwell.

Sheriff Thralls and eight others stayed to examine the area. They looked for evidence to help them track the cowboys. Those who stayed with Thralls were Deputy Frank Evans, R.W. Harrington, John W. (or Jim) Dobson, George D. Freeman, Abram Rhodes, Tell Walton, and Sam Swayer. Thralls continued his search for Talbot for more than a week before giving up temporarily.

On Tuesday, December 27, 1881, George S. Brown, who would become Caldwell's next marshal by March 1882, led another posse in search of Talbot. He headed toward Cantonment in Indian Territory on a tip from freighters. He, too, had no success.

Romantic Interlude

Shortly after his second term as sheriff started, Joe Thralls decided to put his bachelor life behind him. In his time spent as sheriff visiting Caldwell, he had become well acquainted with a number of people who served in his posse. Among them was Caldwell businessman R. W. Harrington. Thralls soon became just as interested in Harrington's daughter as in Harrington himself. Shortly after Harrington served with Thralls in trying to catch Mike Meagher's killer Jim Talbot, Thralls unexpectedly carried out his personal wish for a wife.

Harrington's daughter, Fannie K., was herself an independent sort of woman. She had been a schoolteacher for several years when Thralls met her. Unknown to the public, he courted her and asked for her hand in marriage. She said yes.

The event took place on Sunday, January 15, 1882 in Caldwell. "Rev. J.S. McClung ran an attachment upon Sheriff Joseph M. Thralls last Sunday by uniting him in the holy bonds of wedlock to Miss Fannie K. Harrington, one of Caldwell's fairest maidens," said the Caldwell paper. "The ceremony was performed at the residence

of the bride's father, R.W. Harrington, Esq., and in the afternoon the
newly wedded pair left for Wellington."[6]

Wellington citizens as well were surprised, if not shocked. "Joe
had been arrayed in his good clothes on Monday, but no one thought
that it was because he had been getting married," the Wellington
paper said, "but it seems . . . that such was the case. What a nice
little trick he played on us all, to be sure . . . We hope [Mrs.
Thralls] may pass down the much talked of flower strewn pathway
of life, hand in hand always remembering with happiness, the day
on which she conquered he, who has made a great reputation as a
capturer of others."[7]

11

"I'm Thralls and I want you."

On Thursday morning, June 22, 1882, Caldwell citizens came to Marshal George Brown about three men who had ridden in from Texas. The two roughest looking characters were brothers. Contrary to a city ordinance, they were armed.

Brown asked his deputy, Willis Metcalf, to go with him. They headed to the Red Light Saloon where the two brothers, Edward and James Bean (alias Jess and Steve Green), were spending time. Some of the Red Light patrons spotted the lawmen headed their way and told the Bean brothers.

Inside the Red Light, Marshal Brown and Deputy Metcalf walked upstairs where the three visitors stood. One of the Texans held a pistol. Brown went up to him, grabbed his arm, and asked for the pistol.

"Let go of me," one of the Bean brothers yelled. Brown slammed Bean's arm against a wall.

Meantime another man grabbed Metcalf by the throat and backed him into a corner. Suddenly another man came out of a room across the hall and called out to Brown, "Turn him loose."

This distracted Brown for a moment. It was long enough for Bean to twist his arm, aim the pistol at Brown's head, and fire. Brown fell limp to the floor, stone dead.

The Bean brothers escaped south. Lawmen later learned they were herders for cattle owned by a man named Ellison and a boss named McGee located near Deer Creek. A posse tried to catch them but failed.

The Caldwell paper painted a grim picture of what the reporters first saw at the crime scene. It left a vivid image.

"We found the body of George Brown at the head of the stairs," the editor said, "his face covered with a clot of blood and his brains spattered on the wall and floor of the building, while gore dripped through the floor to the rooms below. Dr. Hume had been called in and was engaged in washing off the blood in order to ascertain the nature of the wound which had caused Brown's death."[1]

Thralls Appeals to Governor

When Sheriff Thralls heard about this, he became incensed with the continuing violence and murder that came from Caldwell. This time he figured he needed to go a step further than he had in the past. He sent a letter to Kansas Governor John P. St. John. In it he told Governor St. John the details of Brown's murder and the recent history of killings in Caldwell. He concluded by saying:

"Now are you not authorized to offer a reward of $500 apiece for their [the Bean brothers] arrest and delivery to the Sheriff of Sumner County? We are having so much of this kind of work it does seem as though the State should offer a good reward for some of these 'Texas killers' and outlaws. This is the fourth murder within the last year at Caldwell and Hunnewell and no reward offered by State for any of them. Yours truly J.M. Thralls, Sheriff. Please answer."

A few days later the Governor answered. He signed a proclamation dated July 6, 1882 from Topeka, Kansas offering $500 "for the arrest and conviction of the said Jeff Green and Steve Green."[2] Sheriff Thralls added $400 to the Governor's offer.[3]

Thralls spread the word about the two desperadoes throughout Indian Territory, New Mexico, Colorado and into Texas.[4] He included the Bean brothers' descriptions as detailed in the coroner's inquest. Jess Green [Ed Bean] was "about five feet ten inches in height, strong built, weighed about 180 pounds; full, broad face, dark complexion; hair black, coarse and straight, mustache and imperial colored black, but naturally of a sunburnt color. Had on dark clothes, leggings, and new white felt had with a leather band around the crown."

His brother Steve Green [James Bean] was "about five feet six or eight inches high, heavy built, coarse black hair, mustache and imperial dyed, broad face, very dark; dressed about the same as his brother, save that his hat was not new."[5]

By spreading the news about the outlaws, getting Governor St. John to offer a reward, and adding to that reward, Joe Thralls did more than he had ever done previously to catch a fugitive. By now he had learned to use the full power of his position as sheriff.

◊

But he still had other business to take care of. He had to conduct sheriff's sales. This began to consume more of his time. Later it would become a subject for some of his critics.

Thralls had other criminals to deal with besides Talbot and the Bean brothers. Often he now worked with other lawmen in his pursuits. One of his favorite lawmen was Cowley County Sheriff Albert Taylor Shenneman. They had much in common (see following chapter for details).

Sometime during the second week of September 1882 Joe Thralls and Al Shenneman got caught off-guard with their prisoner. It happened while they were hauling a desperado named Dick Glass to the Cherokee Nation in Indian Territory.

At about 9 p.m. on their third night of travel, the lawmen spotted a ranch not far distant. They figured this would be a good place to rest for the night. As they approached it, the unexpected happened.

"Glass sprang from the wagon and rushed for a thick patch of underbrush near the road," said the Cowley County paper. "The prisoner was shackled hand and foot and, as the sheriffs thought, perfectly secure. [Glass] was sitting between them, and his actions were so quick that he was two rods away before [Thralls and Shenneman] got their revolvers on him.

"[Thralls and Shenneman] fired twice each, but failed to bring [Glass] down... He left a part of the shackles in the wagon... He had filed them nearly in two between the jams before leaving the [Winfield] jail, and had, by rubbing his feet together, broken them apart."

This was one of the more embarrassing incidents the two sheriffs would have to live down. But it was a rare occurrence.

"Glass has accomplished a feat that few men would care to attempt," said the paper. "The chances were desperate, but the man was equal to the attempt, and escaped from two of the shrewdest and bravest officers in this or any other state. Sheriff Shenneman feels badly over losing the prisoner and the $500 reward which he was to get."[6]

Another Talbot Search

On Tuesday, September 19, Sheriff Thralls headed south into Indian Territory on some previously unsettled business. Sources had told him where the Jim Talbot cowboys involved in Mike Meagher's death were holding stolen cattle. Now Sheriff Thralls and Sheriff Shenneman along with Henry Newton Brown and other lawmen rode south after the Talbot bunch. Henry Brown had been appointed Caldwell's assistant marshal to Marshal B.P. "Bat" Carr on July 3 but resigned temporarily in September to go with Thralls on the manhunt.[7]

The Thralls posse rode south to the Cheyenne-Arapaho agency (present Concho). There Sheriff Thralls talked to Agent John D. Miles, who loaned Thralls a detachment of troops to join them in their search for the Talbot gang. Thralls also learned that at least two of the Talbot cowboys, Doug Hill and Bob Munson, had been spotted at Kooch's camp, which was about 60 miles southwest of the agency. Hill was using the alias Bob Johnson and Munson that of Slocum.

The posse left the agency hopeful of catching their fugitives. Some 20 miles from Kooch's, they came to Seger's camp. There Seger convinced Thralls to stay where he was. Seger would ride to Kooch's and see if the fugitives were still there.

Two days later Seger returned saying he talked to Bob Johnson and decided Johnson didn't fit Doug Hill's description. Thralls didn't accept Seger's explanation. He preferred to confirm it himself.

The Thralls party headed to Kooch's camp. But it was too late. Both Hill and Munson had flown the coop.[8]

Sheriff Tracks Killer Beans

In October Joe Thralls saw the fruit of his labor toward the continuous pursuit of the Bean brothers. It had been four months since the Beans had killed Caldwell Marshal George Brown, but Sheriff Thralls was a patient man. He knew he had done all he could by writing the governor, informing lawmen throughout the area about the Bean brothers, and staying on an alert for any information related to the case.

Since returning to Texas, the Bean brothers had gotten in trouble with the law in Smith County, so they moved to Wise, County. But in Wise County a man followed the trail of someone who had killed one of his cows. The trail led to the Bean brothers. Soon a constable and his posse followed their trail.

On Monday, October 9, the constable caught up with their horses, then hid and waited for the brothers to appear. Jim Bean returned and was within 10 steps of the constable when the lawman jumped up, leveled his shotgun at the outlaw, and called out for him to hold up his hands.

Bean lifted his hands half way, then pulled out a pistol and fired. The bullet glanced off the constable's head knocking him out momentarily. The constable quickly regained consciousness and ran after Bean who was fleeing. Problem was, the constable forgot to pick up his shotgun.

The posse started firing at Bean. One of the bullets struck him in the back. As he fell, Ed Bean appeared carrying two shotguns and a Winchester. That stopped the posse in its tracks. The Beans then escaped.

Ed and Jim Bean traveled eight or 10 miles till they got near their parents' camp but kept in hiding. The lawmen then used a boy who could easily hide to follow the outlaws' trail. He followed them for two days, hiding in bushes and gullies, till he found them. He then snuck back to the constable with the information. It was Wednesday, October 11.

This time the constable and posse quietly surrounded the camp. When all were ready, the constable stepped in clear view of the brothers who were lying on the ground, and holding his shotgun, told them to surrender. He got no response. He asked a second, then a third time.

Suddenly both brothers jumped to their feet and fired their shotguns. They missed their target. The constable yelled, "Turn her loose, boys," and gunfire filled the air. Two bullets riddled Ed Bean's head, killing him instantly. Fourteen bullets found their mark in Jim Bean's body. He had bullets in his back, leg, chest, even one in his head, which knocked him out. Still he remained alive and soon regained consciousness.

Joe Thralls sent Deputy Frank Evans to Texas to bring back Jim Bean. On Wednesday, October 18, Deputy Evans left Decatur, Texas with his prisoner.[9]

Jim Bean died on Sunday morning, November 5, 1882. Sheriff Thralls then sent another letter to Governor St. John, telling him the details of the capture and death of both outlaws. He closed the letter by asking the governor how to go about getting the reward.

"Now what is necessary for us to do to get the State reward – which goes to their captors in Texas?" Thralls asked. "We are asking this for the Texas Officers who have done good work in the case – and what was dangerous work, in good faith, and at some expense. Now I would like to see them rewarded to make our part of the contract good."[10]

As the Caldwell marshal murder case closed, Joe Thralls learned of trouble brewing in Hunnewell. Cowboys were becoming increasingly obnoxious in that newly opened border cow town.

Hunnewell Capture

On Saturday, November 11, 1882, Joe and his brother Elzy went to Hunnewell to see if they could help with the town's law and order problem. Joe figured they might just run into someone they knew that needed confinement since his sources told him so.

He had heard that August Shafecater, alias Ben Butler and nicknamed "Arkansas," was at Hunnewell that day. Shafecater was wanted for cattle stealing in Hays County, Texas.

That night the brothers entered Dodd's Saloon. They asked around and found out Shafecater was in a back room gambling. Joe and Elzy entered the room. It was filled with cowboys.

Joe spotted Shafecater playing cards at the gambling table. Elzy stood at the door while Joe walked around the table behind Shafecater. The sheriff then placed his hand on Shafecater's shoulder. "Come out to the sidewalk," he said. "I want to speak to you."

"I don't know that I will," Shafecater answered. "Who are you?"

"I'm Thralls and I want you."

The roomful of cowboys gathered around the two men. They didn't like what they saw.

Shafecater reached for his gun. Thralls grabbed his hand. They struggled. Thralls by then had cocked his own gun and was ready. He fired it. The crowd scattered and headed outside.

Shafecater stood up, held up his hands, and gave up. Two cowboys near the door stood in Joe's way. They told Joe he'd better not arrest Shafecater.

Elzy then played his part. He held his gun on them and told them to put their hands up. They complied.

Joe handcuffed Shafecater and the Thralls brothers hauled him to the town hotel. They spent the night there and left in the morning. Some cowboys still wanted to rescue Shafecater but their boss convinced them otherwise.[11]

◊

Joe Thralls, now well known for his persistence, continued his search for Talbot whenever he received tips of his location. In January 1883 he posted reward notices with descriptions of some of the cowboys.[12]

12

Friendship as strong as brotherhood

Joe Thralls entered his last year as sheriff hoping he could bring
a little more peace and order to Sumner County. He knew he could
expect more trouble from Caldwell and Hunnewell. Cowboys on
cattle drives went by their own rules and didn't like others butting in
even if they were lawmen.

Sheriff Thralls had learned much from past experiences and
brought that knowledge to his last year. He had learned better how
to gather information on outlaws and distribute that information to
other areas, often leading to arrests. He had learned the hard way to
be vigilant at every moment when handling prisoners.

One of his best talents had to do with his ability to work with
other lawmen in chasing down criminals. His position as U.S.
Deputy Marshal helped. He had contacts throughout surrounding
states and this served him well in catching fugitives. He had made
some close friends among nearby lawmen.

Perhaps one of the closest was Albert Taylor Shenneman, sheriff
of Cowley County, which bordered Sumner to the east. Thralls and
Shenneman traveled thousands of miles together as fellow lawmen
tracking fugitives. They held much in common.

Albert Shenneman came from Illinois to Winfield, Kansas in late
1869. The 24-year-old (born April 10, 1846 in Ohio) was a big
man, six feet one and a half inch tall. He worked as a freighter at
first. He also found other jobs, such as working at Stewart &

Simpson's Brickyard, to support himself in whatever way he could. By May of 1873 he had become Winfield City Marshal.[1] He continued as a lawman the rest of his life.

He became a Republican candidate for Cowley County Sheriff in August 1873 without success. He resigned his position as marshal in September when he ran for sheriff. Since he didn't hold either job, he spent part of the winter hunting buffalo.

On April 3, 1874 he was elected Winfield Township Constable along with Burt Covert. In May he helped Sheriff Richard L. "Dick" Walker arrest horse thief Al Headrick, who stole a horse a few miles southwest of Parsons, Kansas and took it past Grouse Creek a few miles north of Winfield.[2]

To supplement his income, Shenneman sometimes bought horses at government livestock sales in Indian Territory. Other times he went to sales in nearby states such as Arkansas, Texas, of Missouri. He would bring the livestock back to Winfield and sell them for a profit.[3]

In August 1877 Al Shenneman again became a Republican candidate for Cowley County Sheriff.[4] In September, the local paper commented on Shenneman's qualities.

Shenneman "is in every way well qualified for the position [of sheriff]," it said. "In his long career in this county in business of the same nature as are the duties of sheriff, he has proved himself to be honorably and eminently efficient. He has hosts of friends."[5]

Republicans divided on their candidate for sheriff. They voted for two sets of delegates, one favoring Walker, the other, Shenneman. After numerous ballots, Shenneman came out on the short end.[6]

In April 1878 Shenneman, along with Frank Millspaugh, started the Shenneman & Millspaugh Livery Stable in Winfield. In April 1879 Millspaugh sold out his share to A.G. Wilson.[7] In May, Shenneman sold his part "to devote his time to harvesting his 150 acres of wheat in Vernon Township and improving his fine farm."[8]

By late May and early June people were hoping Al Shenneman would become the next sheriff. "Mr. A. T. Shenneman is the choice of the Republican voters of Richland Township," the Winfield paper said. "We want . . . a man who has been tried in the capture of horse and other thieves to the satisfaction and interest of the citizens of Cowley County and A. T. Shenneman is that man."[9]

In July Shenneman agreed to run for sheriff. On the 20th of that month he married Ella C. Walters, also from Winfield and seven years younger.[10]

In September he became the Republican candidate for sheriff.[11] But he had stiff competition from Charles L. Harter, who had served as sheriff the last two years and hoped to be re-elected. Throughout the campaign the two candidates battled for the vote. Harter accused Shenneman of illegal activities and Shenneman accused Harter of negligence in his duties as sheriff.

On November 4 Albert T. Shenneman won, becoming Cowley County's sixth sheriff. He wasted no time in carrying out his duties. On Sunday, November 16, he hunted down Frank Shock who had assaulted someone with a knife. He tracked him all the way to Chautauqua County, captured him, and brought him back to Winfield. This arrest was enough for the paper to say "we have the right man in the right place, and . . . evil doers in the future may expect to be brought to justice."[12]

Toward the end of December 1879, Shenneman arrested Dick Rhonimus, proprietor of the North End Meat Market, and his hired hand Henry, for stealing cattle. Rhonimus was accused of systematically stealing livestock over a period of time. On Wednesday, February 4, Rhonimus and two others escaped from the county jail under suspicious circumstances. One was recaptured the next morning.[13]

In 1881 he captured two horse thieves. They had stolen horses in Labette County. Shenneman returned them to Chetopa on Friday, May 28, but soon found his work was not done.

"After turning his prisoners over to the proper authorities," the paper said, "[Shenneman] learned that the 'Vigilantes' were gathering and intended to hang the prisoners that night. He imparted this knowledge to the constable; but that officer, not seeming to heed the warning, prompted Sheriff Shenneman to take the prisoners around a back alley, get them into a hack, and [Shenneman] drove them to Oswego without being interrupted. He afterwards learned that about twelve o'clock that night, a large party of men surrounded the jail and their cuss words were long and loud when they found that their prey had flown."[14]

By June 1881 Sheriff Shenneman's efficiency in arrests left the county jail nearly full. Of the six prisoners incarcerated, the most famous one was Richard Lennix, a big time forger who used several aliases, among them George Haywood and St. Clair. Shenneman went after him after he along with a partner, Jacob Gross, tried to cash forged drafts for $500 each at the Winfield Bank, the Kohn Brothers' Bank, and Woodman's Bank in April 1880. When Shenneman learned that Lennix was in Chicago, he sent a picture of the man to lawmen in that area, which led to Lennix' arrest.

Lennix had spent time in the Illinois Penitentiary before Shenneman caught up with him. The Winfield paper went into some of the details of the story of Shenneman's success in catching the forger.

"Shenneman went to Chicago, and through many difficulties, got his prisoner, and started home with him," the paper reported. "On the way, the prisoner jumped from the train in full headway and escaped. Shenneman had taken from [Lennix'] pockets a letter written in a female hand from Canton, Illinois, and signed 'S.' By means of this letter, he found who 'S' was and concluded that sooner or later Lennix would visit this 'S,' who was his sister. So he employed the post master at Canton, the marshal of Canton, and the sheriff of that county to watch for him.

"Last week he got a telegram from the sheriff informing him that the prisoner was caught. Shenneman answered at once to hold on to him until he got there, and started for that place. *Habeas Corpus* proceedings were instituted for procuring the prisoner's discharge, and when Shenneman arrived, the *Habeas Corpus* was being heard before the County judge, who soon discharged the prisoner.

"Shenneman grabbed him at once and there was a row, the judge leading the mob and threatening due vengeance on Shenneman. By rapid motions and strategic generalship, Shenneman got his prisoner slipped into a wagon behind the fastest team that could be procured, and putting the horses to their best speed, rushed through opposing crowds and escaped, followed by many pursuers.

"He beat them all in the race and got his prisoner to a station 20 miles distant, put him on board, and sped back to Winfield, where he has his bird safe within the walls of the Cowley County jail."[15]

Sheriff Shenneman stayed on the lookout for Lennix' partner, Jacob Gross. On Thursday, July 21, 1881, he returned from Watertown, Wisconsin with Gross.

These arrests, said the paper, "have given Mr. Shenneman a wide reputation as an efficient officer and a shrewd detective."[16]

Monday, October 17, 1881, at about 8:30 p.m. Thomas J. Armstrong pulled out a six-shooter and killed James Riely, who owned a drug store in Arkansas City. Wednesday morning, October 19, Sheriff Shenneman went to Arkansas City from Winfield and put up a wanted poster, offering $100 reward for the capture of Armstrong. The poster described Armstrong in detail. Shortly after that Shenneman and his posse captured the fugitive.[17]

"Our sheriff is making one of the brightest records of any officer in the state," said the Winfield paper. "His reputation as a vigilant officer is already passed beyond the bounds of our county and has become known all over the state. His exploit of Tuesday adds another laurel to his crown.

"He was notified of the killing of Riely about daylight on the morning of the 18th. He immediately left for Arkansas City, where he went to work. Parties of mounted men were scouring the country in every direction already.

"The Sheriff set quickly to work gathering clues and taking his bearings, paying no attention to the excited rumors floating around. This took some time and the people began to get restless and wonder 'why in thunder the Sheriff didn't go after him.' Shenneman had thrown all his energy and ability into this chase, and with a knowledge of the actions of criminals and the best mode of catching them, was carefully weaving a chain about the case that was sure of success.

"He meant that it should not be a 'wild goose chase,' and it wasn't. By eleven o'clock he had settled in his own mind the direction the murderer had gone and about where he could be found. He then quietly ate his dinner, fed his team, got his posse together, and started.

"He didn't fool around hunting through brush piles and following old roads, but drove straight to the house of Tom Robinson, on Grouse Creek; told Tom that Armstrong had been there that morning, and was somewhere in the vicinity at that moment, scattered his posse out, surrounded the nearest thicket, secured his man, and drove into Arkansas City by four o'clock."[18]

Armstrong was later found guilty of second-degree murder. He was sentenced to 15 years in the penitentiary.

In was no wonder Albert Shenneman easily won a second term. His popularity in Cowley County matched that of Joe Thralls in Sumner. Both began their second term on a very high note. Both increasingly worked together. In 1882 they traveled throughout southern Kansas and Indian Territory tracking outlaws, hauling them back to Sumner or Cowley County or on to Fort Smith, Arkansas, depending on where the crime took place.

In January 1883 Sheriff Shenneman received information about another fugitive on the run. The fugitive, Charles Cobb, was wanted for murder.

On Saturday, January 13, Cobb attended a country-dance in Jefferson County (northeast of Topeka). At the dance, Cobb brandished a knife and gun. A constable tried to arrest Cobb. But Cobb drew his gun and shot the man. The constable died almost instantly.

Cobb escaped going southwest. Most figured he was headed to Hunnewell on his way to the Chisholm Trail and south into Indian Territory.

Sheriff Shenneman received a telegram saying to be on the lookout for a fugitive who was headed his direction. Shenneman then handed out notices describing the fugitive and offering a reward for his capture. The description said Cobb was "about nineteen or twenty years old; light complexion; no whiskers or mustache; blue eyes; a scar over eye or cheek, don't know which; height five to five feet three inches; weight 125 to 130 pounds; had black slouch hat, dark brown clothes, and wore large comforter; may have large white hat; was riding a black mare pony with roach mane, and carried a Winchester rifle and two revolvers; had downcast look."[19]

On Monday morning, January 15, Cobb was spotted in Winfield. From there he headed north toward Udall. A farmer in Vernon Township saw him reading his own wanted poster that Sheriff Shenneman had distributed.

That evening Cobb stopped at Walter Jacobus' farm in Maple Township north of Udall and asked for work, claiming to be an unemployed cowboy. Jacobus had no work to offer but took him in as a boarder anyway. Cobb said his name was George T. Smith. He remained at Jacobus' farm the rest of that week.

On Sunday, January 21, several boys threw bottles in the air for Cobb to shoot as target practice. A schoolteacher, who also boarded at the Jacobus farm, got wind of the incident and figured out the cowboy staying with Jacobus and doing the shooting was none other than the wanted man. He went to Shenneman with the information. Shenneman advised him to get a closer look at the man's face and come back with information to confirm his beliefs. The schoolteacher never returned to Shenneman with more information. But Shenneman still believed the boarder calling himself Smith was Cobb.

Jacobus may also have noticed the wanted poster himself. He too may have told Shenneman he suspected "Smith" to be Cobb.[20]

Sheriff Shenneman still wasn't completely sure, so he decided to go to the farm without a posse and under disguise as a Doctor Jones.

He hoped to see the man close up and catch him off guard if it was Cobb.

On Tuesday morning, January 23, Shenneman rode to the Jacobus farm. He arrived as Jacobus, Jacobus' wife, and Cobb were finishing lunch. Jacobus introduced Shenneman as Dr. Jones from Udall.

One look at the armed stranger and Shenneman knew it was Cobb. Shenneman waited for his chance. Mr. and Mrs. Jacobus, along with Cobb finished lunch. Cobb then stood up, turned around, and went to the front door to leave.

Shenneman saw his chance. He jumped Cobb from behind. They struggled together for some time. Two shots rang out.

During this time Jacobus entered the struggle and subdued Cobb. He grabbed the gun and put a rope around Cobb's neck, choking him till he quit fighting. He then held the gun on Cobb threatening to shoot him if he tried to escape.

"When Shenneman jumped on [Cobb]," said Walt Jacobus, "I followed up close and as soon as I could, I got hold of his revolver and held it on him until he said he would give up. I then called the teacher from the schoolhouse and we tied him."

But it was too late for Shenneman. He had two wounds in the right side of his stomach.

"Hold him, he's killed me," Shenneman gasped. Shenneman made it to the bedroom where he lay down on the bed.[21]

That evening Deputy Taylor and Under-Sheriff George H. McIntyre put Cobb in the sheriff's buggy and headed to Winfield. By then neighbors found out what was going on. One mile outside of Winfield vigilantes tried to overtake the lawmen. But the lawmen outran them.

The lawmen entered Winfield in a roundabout way. McIntyre hid the prisoner in a woodshed while Taylor scouted out the jail. From hiding, Taylor saw vigilantes surrounding the jail. Vigilantes continued to roam about Winfield that night. McIntyre and Taylor somehow managed to keep Cobb in hiding.

Wednesday afternoon, January 24, lawman Deputy Finch took Charles Cobb to the Wichita jail for safekeeping. Thursday morning, January 25, Jefferson County Sheriff Brown, along with a farmer who knew Cobb, arrived in Wichita. The farmer positively identified "Smith" as Charles Cobb.

At 9:45 that evening, Sheriff Shenneman died in Udall. Cobb spent the next day and night in the Wichita jail. At the same time, local residents, now more incensed than ever, planned how to capture him.

Town leaders knew what could happen and called on the most dependable lawmen available to put a stop to lynch law. Sheriff Thralls, together with Sedgwick County Sheriff Hugh R. Watt (Walt?) and Cowley County Deputy Taylor, kept guard over Charles Cobb and headed back to Winfield with him on Saturday morning, January 27. It's not clear why they thought this would offer better protection to Cobb than to have him stay in Wichita. It could have been that no town wanted him because of the trouble he might bring, so Winfield got him by default.

As the lawmen were hauling Cobb back to Winfield, passengers on a northbound train between Udall and Mulvane spotted them. This meant the lawmen would have to hide their prisoner again.

Thralls, Watt, Taylor, and Cobb entered Winfield from an unexpected location. Deputy Taylor scouted out the situation at the jail. He saw crowds of avengers around it ready to grab Cobb. He reported this to the others.

Sheriff Thralls and Sheriff Watt then took Cobb out of the carriage and headed south on foot to some hiding place. They told Deputy Taylor ride off in the carriage in another direction.

Vigilantes soon spotted the carriage, stopped it, and demanded that Taylor tell where the prisoner was. He held out long enough for Sheriff Thralls and Sheriff Watt to get away.

It was after two a.m. before the sheriffs found a carriage to take Cobb to safety. Watt ended up taking Cobb back to Wichita by way of Douglass while Thralls returned to Winfield.

143

Later that day, Sunday afternoon, January 28, Sheriff Thralls attended Albert T. Shenneman's funeral at the First Baptist Church in Winfield. The funeral attracted an astoundingly large crowd. The Winfield paper said it "brought together the largest congregation of people ever seen on a like occasion in Southern Kansas."[22]

One lawman stood out from the rest as Shenneman's close friend. "There was Sheriff Thralls, of Sumner," said the Winfield paper, "with whom Sheriff Shenneman had traveled thousands of miles and through many dangerous ways in pursuit of criminals and between whom there existed a personal friendship as strong as brotherhood."[23]

Numerous other law officers attended the funeral. Of the sheriffs alone there was Butler County Sheriff W. H. Douglass (brother of the town founder); Elk County Sheriff W. I. Thompson; Chautauqua County Sheriff William Boyd; Montgomery County Sheriff William Lafayette "Lafe" Shadley (who later gained fame chasing down Bill Doolin gang members and dying in a shootout in Ingalls, Oklahoma); Cowley County Sheriff George H. McIntyre (who had replaced Shenneman); and Jefferson County Sheriff Brown who had helped identify Charles Cobb. Sedgwick County Sheriff Hugh R. Watt would have been there had he not been watching his prisoner, Charles Cobb.

Four special trains from Wellington, Arkansas City, Newton, and Wichita brought people to the funeral. Six sheriffs carried the coffin to the front of the church before the funeral ceremony.

In his sermon, the minister, Rev. J.E. Platter, asked citizens not to seek vengeance. He "referred to the kind and generous spirit of the dead Sheriff; how he would go almost any length, and imperil his own life, to save even the most hardened criminal from harm, and himself from shedding human blood; and how almost his last request was to protect his murderer from violence. The minister then put the question squarely to the people: Should they emulate the spirit and desire of their dead friend or allow the spirit of vengeance to overcome them and resort to violence toward his murderer? The effect of the discourse was powerful; and strong men, who had gone there determined that, as soon as their honored friend was laid beneath the sod, his murderer should expiate the crime with his life, went away feeling that it was better to let the law takes its course."[24] Rev. Bicknell, editor of the *Chicago Advocate*, said the closing prayer.

The funeral procession to Union Cemetery in Winfield showed how highly local residents valued their former sheriff. The procession stretched out for more than a mile long.

As much as the minister wanted justice to run its course, a group of citizens didn't. Or at least they saw justice in a different light.

Charles Cobb still remained in the Wichita jail hoping for some reprieve, or at least a trial. He knew how local citizens felt. He spent a restless Sunday and Monday night there. On Tuesday evening, Deputy Taylor headed back to Winfield with Cobb. He got lost on the way and didn't arrive till the next day.

On Wednesday, January 31, Deputy Taylor delivered Cobb to the Winfield jail. Taylor and William Shenneman, the dead sheriff's brother who was a law officer in Bay City, Michigan, helped Sheriff McIntyre watch the prisoner that night. That same evening Mrs. Albert Shenneman came to the jail and talked to Cobb. At 11 p.m. Cobb admitted who he was and what he did. He said he had gone down the wrong path from reading about Jesse James and others.

Shortly after two a.m. (Thursday, February 1) Sheriff McIntyre ran into trouble. By then William Shenneman and Deputy Taylor had left the jail to sleep in a house across the street. The town had been quiet all evening. McIntyre was relaxing by the stove.

Suddenly someone jimmied open the front door and burst in. Outside stood 12 to 14 men, at least four with drawn guns. The leader told McIntyre, "Throw up your hands." McIntyre complied.

"If he moves a hand, put a whole through him," the leader told the armed men. The vigilantes got the key from McIntyre, opened the cell, and removed the prisoner. Several men held McIntyre at bay for about five minutes while the rest left with Cobb. All the vigilantes wore masks made of black cloth with eyeholes in them.

Meantime Deputy Taylor heard noise from the jail and rushed to the scene only to stop when several vigilantes held him up at gunpoint. "You beat us Saturday night but you can't do it this time," one of them told him. "We're organized."

The vigilantes carried out their work. McIntyre later found Cobb hanging near the Walnut River. The official inquest concluded that "the said Charles Cobb came to his death on the morning of February first, 1883, by being hung by the neck from the [railroad] bridge of the K. C. L. and S. R. R. across the Walnut River, in Cowley County, Kansas, at the hands of parties unknown to the jury."[25]

This had become a familiar scene to Joe Thralls. Perhaps he felt lucky this time not to be involved in Cobb's death. But the whole affair, from his best friend's death to the lynching, reminded Thralls of the precarious position he held as Sumner County sheriff. He still had a year to serve and the Sumner County border towns still thrived on violence.

13

"We have no enmity."

Sheriff Thralls faced a hard decision little more than a week after Charles Cobb was lynched. In the first week of February 1883 Thralls received news that Charley Davis, the man who killed Caldwell's Red Light Saloon owner George Woods back in August 1881, had been arrested in Albuquerque, New Mexico. Thralls could take custody of Davis in Albuquerque and bring him back to Wellington. Mag Woods offered $500 reward in addition to a reward offered by the governor. But Thralls soon had doubts about getting Davis.

Davis said he wanted to stand trial to prove his innocence. That's when Thralls began putting two and two together. He suspected ulterior motives. When he connected the dots, he backed off from Davis' offer.

The man who "captured" Davis, Lee Stewart, was a hard case himself. Back in February 1871 Stewart had helped Jack Bridges kill Jack Ledford in Wichita. Bridges was acting as a lawman with a warrant for Ledford's arrest when this took place. But many suspected the killing came closer to murder than legal arrest.

Ledford had beat Bridges in a fistfight shortly before this event. Ledford had married and bought a hotel shortly before this event. Others suspected him of being a horse thief. There were enough questions in people's minds about the Ledford killing to suspect Lee Stewart had helped Bridges for reasons other than upholding the law.

Sheriff Thralls thought about how willing Charley Davis was to stand trial. He thought about the kind of man Lee Stewart was. And he thought about the reward offered. He then suspected a conspiracy between the two.

Stewart would get the reward. Davis would probably go Scot-free since most witnesses were no longer available. And more than likely the two would split the reward. When these facts came out, others agreed. The local paper lauded Thralls for his decision.[1]

By 1883 Joe Thralls spent increasing time with legal business of being sheriff rather than hunting down criminals. This included conducting sheriff's sales. These involved transfer of land and property ownership. Sometimes the sales were a daily affair. Thralls' heart wasn't in this but he had to fulfill his responsibilities.

With less time to focus on law enforcement and tracking criminals, Thralls increasingly had to depend on his deputies. With more police work delegated work, he missed out on some action, such as a shootout on Wednesday, April 11.

His brother Elzy, still serving as a deputy, took part in catching some horse thieves after a gun battle on that April day. Joe received the news from Elzy and the other lawmen. The incident began when a Texas man named J.W. Herring (or Herron) asked lawmen in Caldwell for help in arresting horse thieves.

Back in Texas, Herring (Herron) lost two mules and two horses at the hands of these thieves. The group included J.W. Ross, his wife, daughter, sons Samuel and James, a daughter-in-law and her baby, and several others. Herring (Herron) followed them from Texas to a place fives miles southeast of Hunnewell.

Herring (Herron) didn't think he could take on the whole group, so on Sunday, April 8 he headed into Caldwell for help. There he found U.S. Deputy Marshal Cassius M. "Cash" Hollister, who was willing to investigate. The two men rode out to where the horse thieves camped. Hollister saw the situation and decided they needed more help.

Back in Caldwell Hollister hauled in more reinforcements. Caldwell Marshal Henry Newton Brown and his deputy Ben

Wheeler headed back to the campsite with Hollister and Herron at 11 p.m. Tuesday. The posse picked up City Marshal Jackson and Deputy Sheriff Elzy Thralls in Hunnewell. At dawn on Wednesday, April 11 they neared the horse thieves' camp. The posse spread out, surrounding the campsite. A Winchester rifle blast from the camp suddenly pierced the morning stillness. Shots between the parties soon filled the air. Firing continued for about 30 minutes. The lawmen continued till their enemy quit firing. Groans came from the Ross party. Then they surrendered.

Samuel Ross, the older brother, lay dead with a bullet through his head and another through his chest. James Ross lay on the ground moaning. One bullet nearly severed his hand, and two other bullets hit him, one in each knee. Samuel's body was taken to Hunnewell. The other thieves went to jail in Wellington. Joe Thralls was glad his brother and the posse escaped injury.[2]

Clay County, Texas Sheriff King took the prisoners back to Texas. Within a week King wired Joe Thralls that he had caught two more horse thieves in Texas connected with the Ross family.

◊

In the first week of August 1883 Elzy announced he was running for sheriff of Sumner County. He, like Joe, had repeatedly shown his bravery and ability as a lawman. It looked like Elzy would be the overwhelming favorite in the next election.

Joe still dealt with crime directly when he had time. Ever since becoming sheriff, Thralls had confronted John W. Griffith. Griffith had served as Wellington city treasurer before he got in debt from gambling and then got in trouble from forging checks. In the first few months Thralls served as sheriff, Griffith was one of his prisoners. Since then he had been in trouble with the law.

Early in August he again had to go after John Griffith. He was wanted for a number of forgeries. "Griffith's forgeries were on James Matthews for $100 and S. L. Hamilton for $357," said the Sumner County Press. "He had already made way with $2,100

149

belonging to Jacob Allen, $1,000 belonging to L. Keys, and $250 belonging to Mr. Packard, of London Township."

Joe Thralls went to Griffith's father's house next to the Chikaskia River. There he found Griffith hiding out in a trunk and arrested him.[3]

Meantime trouble had been brewing for the last several weeks in Hunnewell. It had become a rowdy cow town that matched Caldwell for the cattle trade and cowboys wanting to celebrate. In July, town leaders had asked Sheriff Thralls for help. Thralls found a man for the job. It was Joe Forsythe, a Texan with 12 years experience as a lawman in tough towns. Forsythe chose another Texan, Hamilton Raynor, as his deputy. But neither had arrived yet when trouble came that August.

Among the many cattlemen who frequented Hunnewell regularly were the Halsell brothers, Oscar and Harry, who ran the 4D Ranch a few miles northeast of present day Guthrie. On Thursday, August 9, 4D cowboys began celebrating in Hunnewell, drinking whiskey and shooting randomly. Cowboys from the 3 Circle Ranch in Texas, run by Glenn Halsell (Oscar and Harry's uncle), soon joined them. Their celebration continued for three days. The third day, some townspeople used their recently installed telephone line between Hunnewell and Wellington to call Sheriff Thralls for help. They couldn't wait for Forsythe.

This time Thralls handled the situation himself. He organized a posse and headed south by special train to the rowdy town. In his posse were his brother Elzy, A.W. Shearman, W.W. Guthrie, Frank Evans, Harry Woods, Horace Meixsell, and Fred Aldrich. Thralls and his men arrived 40 minutes later, at 4:15 p.m.

When the Halsell brothers, who stayed hidden from sight, saw the lawmen getting off the train, Oscar wanted to shoot them on sight, but backed off. The lawmen began arresting cowboys, using the town hotel as a holding cell.

Oscar slipped away to the livery stable to saddle horses for his brother and himself. At the stable two members of the posse tried to arrest him but he refused, threatening to shoot it out rather than give in. The two men let him go.

Harry out of curiosity went to the hotel to see what was going on. The posse arrested him.

The Sumner County paper mentioned Joe Thralls' role in the arrests. "A force was organized and nine of the cowboys rounded up," it said. "One of the lot was a stray, however, and only eight of them, R.A. Mitchell, A.T. Mitchell, Dick Weston [West], Powell Wood, Thad Standard, Harry Hosell [Halsell], Frank McClaskey and Joe Garner were taken to Wellington. Bob Mitchell resisted arrest and ran at Thralls with a knife, but Thralls knocked him down and he subsided."[4]

The next day the cowboys paid their fines and Joe Thralls released them. They headed into Indian Territory. But these arrests didn't end the reign of reckless cowboys in Hunnewell.

Marshal Forsyth and Deputy Raynor had gone to Wellington to report to Sheriff Thralls before going to Hunnewell. Thralls told the two lawmen Hunnewell still had some wild cowboys and needed help as quickly as possible. Thralls also told Forsyth to look for Dick Turner since he served as leader of the 4D cowboys. So Forsyth and Raynor took a train to Hunnewell on Thursday, August 16. They also took deputies Elzy Thralls, Thralls' younger brother, Worth, and W.W. Guthrie with them.

When the posse got to Hunnewell, they went to the town hotel hoping to catch Turner. The Sumner County paper said, "They made a mistake by running out of the hotel and up the street towards a saloon where the outlaw was said to be, without knowing their man by sight. Instead of being in the saloon, Turner was sitting on his horse in the middle of the street.

"When the posse had run by him some one called out that the man on horseback was the one they wanted. Turner and two others who were on horseback immediately put spurs to their horses. Seven shots were fired promiscuously towards the fleeing men. The last shot struck Turner in the left side just as he passed the depot, but he rode off. A load of buckshot struck another man's horse and killed it. Three loads of buckshot passed through Mr. Avery's store, where about twenty men were. One ball struck young James Rhodes under the left arm, broke the skin and blackened the flesh considerably.

"Personally, we did not like the music of stray balls around our cranium and it appears the others did not either, as there was a general stampede, in which we landed, all spraddled out, on top of Mr. Avery's watermelon pile, much to the discomfiture of the aforesaid melons."[5]

After that incident, Joe Forsythe seemed to get everything under control. "Jo. Forsythe, the new marshal of Hunnewell, is reported walking around with nothing to do," said a Wellington paper. "The outlaws don't care about tackling a thoroughbred."[6] This continued through September. But it brought out strong opinions both for and against Forsythe.

Cowboys, as expected, thought Forsythe was a cold-blooded gunfighter willing to kill at the drop of a hat. Some others in Hunnewell tended to agree. But strong law and order advocates thought Forsythe fit the bill perfectly for the Hunnewell cow town. These opinions were based on Forsythe's willingness to use gunplay without hesitation as shown in the August 16 shootout. That incident contrasted sharply with the August 13 incident in which Sheriff Thralls and his men captured eight cowboys without a shot.

Some may have thought Sheriff Thralls went too easy on cowboys. Comments from local papers said as much. "The arrest and punishment of these men with fine and imprisonment may deter others from exhibiting a cowardly disregard for the peace and comfort of the citizens of Hunnewell," said the *Caldwell Journal*, "but somehow the impression still lingers that a coroner's inquest over the remains of two or three of them would have had a more soothing effect upon the exuberance of their spirits."[7]

"It cost them about $400 for their fun," said the *Arkansas City Traveler*, "but had they been imprisoned awhile as well as fined, we believe it would have made more impression upon them."[8]

On the other hand, Joe Forsythe came under such criticism for being trigger happy that he felt compelled to respond to a Wellington newspaper article against him. No doubt part of the criticism came from businessmen who saw a decline in their business when the cowboys were tamed down and consequently spent less money.

"This morning while looking through the columns of your valuable paper my eye was arrested by an article headed, 'Hunnewell Racket,'" wrote Forsythe. "I say without a stutter that his attack upon me and [my] assistant is ungentlemanly and uncalled for.

"I have been for twelve years an officer in frontier towns. I don't seek notoriety as a killer. I am not an advertised bad man; but I am paid by the citizens of Hunnewell to keep order here and I propose to do it in spite of the cheap dude like eloquence of 'His Nibs.' I have all respect for the cowboy and in my many years among them have always found them whole-souled honorable men with no desire to do any wrong or break through the bounds of the law...

"I will say that I was sent for by your worthy sheriff at the instigation of the citizens of Hunnewell. He speaks (His Nibs) of the unwarranted interference of himself and others, between cowboys and citizens of this place. Now if any apology is due for not permitting one man to murder another, I am in a strange land. If an apology is due, why not let Sheriff Thralls make it. But no, people here were frightened; they telegraphed Mr. Thralls and he, faithful officer, came at once, accompanied by some of Wellington's citizens who were to aid him in case he needed assistance in performing his duties...

"I am not a killer and my assistants are not desperado police as we can prove by our letter and credentials from some of the best men of the country where we have been employed; and it rather makes our feet sore to have a howling coyote slobbering forth his puerile drivelings across our pathway."[9]

Political fighting continued in Hunnewell. After several months of it, Marshal Forsythe had had enough. He left his badge behind and headed back to Texas.

As Joe Thralls neared the end of his last term as sheriff, his brother Elzy still seemed to be a shoo-in to replace him. The future looked bright for the Thralls family. Joe Thralls had two other brothers who could serve as lawmen in the future. Worth Thralls, 26 in 1883, had gained some experience as a lawman when he served on posses with Elzy. And there was Edward F. Thralls, one year younger than 33-year-old Elzy.

Unexpected Opponent

Joe's outstanding career as a lawman had opened the door for the rest of his family. Any intelligent observer could see that. No one, least of all the Thralls boys, could have anticipated what would happen to change all this before Joe Thralls ended his time as sheriff.

Sheriff Thralls was blindsided by a fellow Republican. Sumner County Press Editor Andy A. Richards for some reason didn't want another Thralls to replace Joe even though they were fellow Republicans. This seemed to be a complete reversal of how Richards treated Joe Thralls two years earlier.

At that time Richards praised Thralls for how well he performed his duty as sheriff. He supported the sheriff for a second term without question. So what happened between then and this election? That's what many wondered. It would remain a mystery.

In the August 30 issue of the *Sumner County Press*, Andy Richards shocked others, especially other Republicans. He leveled his criticism toward Joe Thralls. But his aim was to stop Joe's brother, Elzy, from becoming sheriff. In an article titled "Wisdom of the Law," Richards began:

"As is generally known, there is a Kansas statute which limits a sheriff's term of office to two terms or four years. This is an important office and one in which large money interests are at stake. The same is true of the county treasurer's office. Therefore, the law provides that at least once in four years an entire change shall be made in these offices and a general settlement be made in consequence.

"To show that this is a wise provision of law, we propose to give a few facts and an abstract from the county records of the district clerk's office.

"We know that Sumner County has had an excellent criminal sheriff in J.M. Thralls and he might have been even a better civil sheriff had he devoted his attention to it himself. We have always said every good word possible for him and his under sheriff and shall continue to do so hereafter. But in view of the fact that another sheriff must be chosen it is only just that the rank and file of the Republicans of the county should know the condition of affairs."

If the last sentence of that third paragraph had substituted "people" for "rank and file of the Republicans" this could have been a perfect introduction for any Democrat hoping to run against the dominant Republicans of Sumner County. What followed would have fit just as well.

In fact, some Republicans may have feared a Democratic victory in November if Elzy Thralls became their candidate. Yet there seemed to be something more than that for Richards to abandon his support for the Thralls family name so thoroughly.

In this article Richards went in detail about sheriff's sales conducted by Joe Thralls between May 6, 1882 and June 9, 1883. He listed 20 separate cases in which he said Thralls had not returned writs of execution within the 60-day limit required by law.

Richards ended the article by trying to say he had the highest of motives. "These facts are published to the public good, especially of the Republican party," he said. "We have no enmity or grudge against J.M. Thralls, nor his proxy, W.E. Thralls."

Anyone in either of the Thralls' positions would have had trouble seeing those high motives in a supposed friend. Blindsided as they were, the Thralls had to figure out some way to respond.

155

Another local paper, the *Wellingtonian*, believed Richards had no motive other than preventing Elzy Thralls from becoming sheriff. The September 6 issue of the *Wellingtonian* ran an article rebutting Richards' arguments. But that same week Richards wrote a second article in the *Sumner County Press* with more accusations.

Richards reviewed what he said in the first article and clarified even further his underlying motive. Because of Joe Thralls' supposed neglect of his duties in finishing the paperwork in sheriff's sales, Richards "argued that the Republicans of this county should not nominate W.E. Thralls for sheriff because that would not be a change in fact." In simple language, Richards unblushingly appealed to guilt by association.

Richards pointed to another case in Kansas where a sheriff was fined for exceeding the 60-day limit before returning a writ. Richards claimed that if Joe Thralls were to be fined for the cases exceeding his 60-day limits, Thralls would be deep in debt. Yet Richards stopped short of calling Thralls' action criminal. He labeled it "neglect" rather than "misconduct." But he wanted to make sure Elzy Thralls didn't receive the Republican nomination, so he concluded this second article by asking Republicans to reject Elzy based on Joe's "neglect."[10]

The *Wellingtonian* (September 6, 1883) meanwhile answered Richards' August 30 piece in an article titled "Vile Attack on a Worthy Officer." The editor quoted from Richards' article before answering the attack.

"It is seldom that a paper making any pretences to respectable journalism willfully slanders a public officer for the mere gratification of personal spite," said the editor, "but the above is one of the few exceptions. The strangest part of it all, however, is that a man can be found so entirely reckless as to make charges of such magnitude without sufficient foundation to even suggest a suspicion of their truthfulness, and many of them being in the very face of the records.

"While it is made the duty of the sheriff to return executions and orders of sale within sixty days, no one denies that under certain circumstances an officer is justified in holding an execution or order of sale more than sixty days without being either criminally liable or derelict in duty and that it is done in hundreds of cases by the best sheriffs in Kansas. We have taken some trouble to investigate these charges and we do not deem any apology necessary for the space it requires to take them up seriatim and give them our attention."

The article reviewed the 20 cases with explanations for each. "Thus it is seen that in 12 of the forgoing cases the records show … that the writs were returned by the sheriff within sixty days from their issuance and in nearly all of them Richards has received his costs," the *Wellingtonian* editor summarized.

"In only eight case have the writs been held more than sixty days, and then by direction of the attorneys managing the cases, as the statement of James Lawrence and McDonald & Parker show as to two of them. In only four cases – the last four referred to by the *Press* – is there any indication of even carelessness. In these cases the costs were paid to the sheriff who turned the orders over to the clerk during the April term of court intending to make the settlements after the adjournment of court as both he and the clerk were busy in court, and they were forgotten. In not a single case has there been the slightest deviation from the strictest integrity and no one has been wronged or defrauded out of a cent."

The editor described Richards' accusations as "a villainous outrage and a silly, puerile attempt to blacken the character of an honest man, and a faithful, efficient officer." He continued "no sheriff or other public functionary ever quitted his office with cleaner hands than will Joseph M. Thralls."

The following week both the *Wellingtonian* and the *Sumner County Press* extended their arguments for and against Thralls. This time Richards dug deeper and painted Joe Thralls as an arrogant lawman who disregarded the law. "He [Thralls] knows just how to run things and does so irrespective of the laws or court to suit his own pleasure and profit and who dares to say him nay?" Richards claimed. "The reckless cuss who does so brings down on his own head the vengeance of the high and mighty Thralls and the

157

money power which stands at his back. Nor should any man interfere when he proposes to evade the law and perpetuate his reign and spoils by being elected by proxy through W.E. Thralls, his brother. The sheriff's office of Sumner County belongs to the Thralls family, and when [Elzy's] four years are out, another one is on the ground in training and when the present supply is exhausted there are plenty more up around Lawrence ready for importation. For one, we are not ready to submit to a Thralls dictatorship."[11]

Joe did come from a big family. Besides Elzy, 33, there were brothers Edward F., 32, Frank W., 30, Worth T., 26, and John, 22, as well as sisters Mollie, 28, Cynthia and Sarah, both 21, and Martha, 17.

Even if Richards' rhetoric exceeded his facts, he hoped it would have the effect he was after – the defeat of Elzy as a candidate for sheriff. He didn't have long to wait. In another week Republican met to choose their candidate.

The very fact that Richards created questions about Thralls abilities as sheriff took its toll on Elzy. Sumner County Republicans divided over his candidacy. After a battle between two competing groups, Elzy lost out to E. Frank Henderson. Andy Richards accomplished his goal. He killed the Thralls "dynasty" before it began. How it affected Joe Thralls could be measured by what followed.

Joe Thralls had another two months to serve as sheriff. He had no control over what Richards had done, but he did over how he filled his position. On Tuesday morning, October 2, he boarded a freight train headed for the penitentiary. He had several prisoners in his custody. They represented a cross section of criminals he had to deal with throughout his career as a lawman.

Among them were John W. Griffith, sentenced to three years for forgery; Charles Davis, sentenced to three years (third degree manslaughter) for killing Caldwell's Red Light Saloon owner George Woods; James Turner, sentenced to three years for grand larceny; and W. F. Gage, sentenced to 18 months for horse stealing.[12]

Griffith served as Wellington city treasurer till the end of 1879 when he ran into trouble after running out of money. Word was he liked to gamble. Whatever the reason, he began cashing bad checks. By early 1880, as mentioned earlier, he had become a prisoner in the Sumner County jail under Elzy Thralls' watchful eyes. From that time till the day Joe Thralls hauled him to the penitentiary he was in and out of trouble.

Davis, it will be remembered, had been caught in Albuquerque, New Mexico back in February, but Thralls had decided not to go after him. Since then he had been returned to Sumner County. Now Davis was headed for hard time.

In November, Frank Henderson left his job as constable to become Sumner County's new sheriff. The township proved they believed the Thralls brothers were still trustworthy lawmen when they appointed Elzy to take Henderson's place as constable.[13] But Elzy's heart wasn't in it. Soon Joe replaced him and began serving another term as constable in 1884. Whether Joe's heart was in it or not, he figured it was his duty to continue in what he knew best. And he still held his position as a U.S. deputy marshal.

14

Civilian Leader

Joe Thralls wasn't one to dwell on the past even though Andy Richards sank Elzy's chances of becoming sheriff. Richards' charges against Joe for incompetence temporarily hurt Joe and pretty well ended Elzy's efforts in Kansas. Joe and Elzy never quite figured out how to counter Richards' charges. As usual, in politics it's much harder to defend against charges than to show positive accomplishments. But life went on.

When Republican E. Frank Henderson was elected Sumner County sheriff, he resigned as constable. Elzy was appointed to replace him.[1] But Elzy had no desire to continue in that role. Soon Joe replaced him.

Now that Joe was no longer sheriff he had more time for family life. As a constable who still held his position as a U.S. deputy marshal, he still worked at what he knew best. In the following years he became a respected city leader and Oklahoma livestock dealer.

After marrying Fannie Harrington in January 1882 he and his bride moved into a place across from the Wellington courthouse. The address was 520 North Washington (at the southwest corner Washington and 11th). Elzy moved to the southwest corner of Chestnut (Olive) and 7th.

Sadly, Joe and Fannie's first child, Lee H., who was born near the end of 1882, died October 25, 1884. Their next two children were daughters; Josephine M. (Josie), born in 1885, and Nettie A., born in 1887. They later had another son, Warren H.

After 1884, Sumner County along with the rest of the country went through changes that put an end to the Wild West era in America. For all practical purposes 1884 was the last year of any significant trail drives from Texas into Kansas.

Land owners' barbed wired shut down the Chisholm Trail, along with the westward moving quarantine line to prevent Texas cattle from mixing with northern domestic herds, and complaints from farmers and ranchers. Local, county, state, and federal law became more organized west of the Mississippi. The remaining wildness that once marked Kansas and especially Sumner County moved further west.

Oklahoma continued to experience outlaw bands such as Bill Doolin's. Wyoming experienced the Butch Cassidy gang. Other outlaws still roamed in Arizona and New Mexico. But these were the dying remnants of a passing era – the era of the once Wild West of cowboys, lawmen, and outlaws.

Joe Thralls also looked to his early days in Wellington as a lawman between 1871 and 1885 as a unique time. As those days closed, so did the memory of his deeds to those around him. Unlike his contemporaries - Wyatt Earp, Wild Bill Hickok, Billy the Kid - he had no newspaper reporters or popular authors drilling him about his dangerous days chasing outlaws, taking part in gunfights, or capturing criminals.

As mentioned, after his days as a lawman, family man Joe Thralls began investing in real estate and became a stock dealer. His real estate holdings eventually included a number of lots in Wellington (three in block 32 and a number of lots in Wellington's Woodlawn addition) and two and a half sections (1,600 acres) in Caddo County, Oklahoma where he raised his livestock. Besides those holdings, he owned 640 acres in San Diego County, California.[2]

By the 1890s, Joe's brother Elzy became a lawman in Oklahoma. Elzy served as a sheriff in Enid, Oklahoma (Garfield County).

Though Joe had interests (and more land) in Oklahoma, he remained a citizen of Wellington, Kansas.

In 1892, Joe Thralls faced a crisis like no other in his life and it had nothing to do with gunfire. A storm brewed on Friday night, May 27. Around 8 p.m. gusts of wind swept through the streets of Wellington. Rain began to fall.

At 8:57 p.m., the wind died down. Sudden calm filled the air. Then townspeople heard a roar approach from the west. Next came chaos. Houses and businesses through the center of town burst apart before the swirling force of a tornado.

Headlines in the June 9, 1892 *Sumner County Standard* read: "Wellington Struck by Death Dealing Tornado - Eleven People Killed and Scores Wounded – Sixteen Blocks in Ruins." Property loss was estimated at $500,000.

Joe Thralls at that time served as manager of the city's water company, and the light and heat company. His house and his company buildings were among the structures destroyed, as was the courthouse across the street from him. He and Fannie escaped injury, but their girls were not so lucky. Josephine, then seven, suffered gashes to her head and thigh, and a mashed foot. Nettie, just five, was badly bruised and had a cut on her shoulder.

Thralls continued to serve as a city leader. The 1906 city directory showed four people living at the Thralls house. They were Joe and Fannie, and their daughters Josie and Nettie. Josie, 21, was listed as a music teacher and Nettie, 19, as a teacher. Josie continued to live with her parents and work as a music teacher through 1921. Warren was listed in the 1915 through 1919 directories as a student living with his parents.

As decades passed, memories of Joe Thralls' early deeds faded. Yet between 1885 and 1917 respect for him never died. That respect came from the character Thralls displayed throughout his life rather than just his early days.

Citizens continued to hold him up as a leader, someone who consistently supported and promoted Wellington and Sumner County. By early 1917, Joe Thralls, 68, decided to run for mayor.

With Thralls' widespread popularity by then, he faced little opposition. The April 4 issue of the *Wellington Monitor-Press* told the story.

"In the city election yesterday [Tuesday, April 3] J.M. Thralls was elected mayor, receiving 740 votes out of a total of 1,024 cast, to 185 for Amos A. Belsley and 99 for A.S. Brubaker. Thralls' name was the only one on the official ballot, he having received the primary nomination without opposition. Mr. Brubaker was the only other avowed candidate.

"Quite a number of voters cast their ballots for ex-Mayor A.A. Belsley, who made no announcement of his candidacy but on whom the opposition to Mr. Thralls centered to a certain extent. The day was a most disagreeable one, the prevailing high winds and dust storm keeping many voters, women especially, from undertaking the trip to the polls. The election was exceedingly quiet, and there was very little employment of autos or other vehicles in bringing voters to the polls..."

Thralls led Wellington for the next 11 years. "Mr. Thralls was elected mayor in 1917 and served out his three years," said the local paper. "He was again appointed mayor to serve out the unexpired term of J.P. Naylor who followed Thralls in office. Again in 1922 he was elected mayor for one year. He came up again for re-election in 1923 and was chosen by the people to serve as their mayor for another three years."[3]

When Thralls began his first term as mayor, the United States was fighting in World War One. Wellington, like communities throughout the country, ended up sending a number of citizens to that cause.

Shortly after the war ended, the town leaders thought of a way to honor the memory of those who had served their country. Mayor Thralls and the city commissioners proposed the idea of a city auditorium that could serve a number of purposes. They saw it as a place that could be used for high school commencements, drama or musical presentations, public meetings, public speeches by famous people, or athletic contests, to name a few functions. This was something the city at the time lacked.

On April 26, 1919, Mayor Thralls and the city commission decided on a location. They purchased land on the west side of Washington Avenue between 7th and 8th Street for $11,350 and decided the building would be called Liberty Hall. Progress on the project moved slowly.

By 1921 they decided to change the name to Memorial Hall. On March 24, 1922, builders laid down the cornerstone. In June the building had progressed to the point of having huge lettering constructed on the front that said "Memorial Hall." On July 26, 1922, the city commission ordered $6,500 worth of seats from American Seating Company. This included 1,250 seats for balconies and 600 folding chairs for the arena. Total cost for the building came to $160,000.

Shortly before the building opened, Mayor Thralls attended the quad county reunion in Mulvane for "Old Settlers." The Wellington paper claimed at least 2,500 gathered for it in the Mulvane Park.

"D.N. Caldwell, Wellington's first mayor, was given a prominent seat on the platform as Exhibit A," it said, "while J.M. Thralls, the present mayor, figured as Exhibit B... Both men are old-timers of high degree, the present mayor in point of residence here antedates by a short time the first mayor."[4]

When the opening ceremony for the memorial auditorium took place on November 19, 1922, people looked in awe at the impressive structure and its interior. A massive stage rigging operated by an intricate switchboard (cost: $1,100) could roll up the stage curtain with its copy of Bartholdi's Statue of Liberty done by Kansas City Scenic Company on it.[5]

The building is still used regularly to this day. Mayor Thralls and the city commission had good reason to take pride in their efforts to bring this attraction to Wellington.

During the early 20s, the town celebrated its 50th anniversary. By then reporters and writers wanted to know more about the early days of Wellington and Sumner County. Mayor Thralls along with his friend William Hackney and other old timers provided that information from memory.

Besides the local paper, newspaperman Tom A. McNeal from Medicine Lodge was old enough to remember something about Thralls' past. And McNeal was also interested in learning more.

He got Joe Thralls to talk about several of his experiences and included them in McNeal's book, *When Kansas Was Young* (1922). More than likely, Thralls' experiences recounted in this book came as a surprise to many of the younger generation. Talking about his early adventures even then didn't come easy to Thralls. His reluctance to exaggerate his experiences was another reason Thralls never received the attention other western lawmen got.

Yet Thralls himself showed great interest in the history he went through. He had an abiding interest in Oklahoma where he had chased outlaws during his youth. He remained a non-resident member of the Oklahoma Historical Society to the end of his life.[6]

Late in 1922 Joe Thralls faced unexpected opposition in his job as mayor. Fred Crabbe, superintendent of the Kansas Anti-Saloon League, and J.R. Codding, a special investigator, accused Mayor Thralls, Wellington City Marshal A.A. Dillon, and his deputy, I.A. Dogget of failing to do their duty as city officials. Crabbe and Codding claimed Thralls failed to enforce the prohibition law in Wellington.

Prohibition had been the law in Kansas since the 1880s. It also became a national law when congress ratified the 18th amendment on January 16, 1919. Since then prohibition groups crusaded for better enforcement of it.

Headlines in December 1922 read, "Bitter Because Outsiders Probe – Wellington Pioneers Defend the Cleanliness of City and Character of Officers." The lead sentence in the article, written by a *Wichita Eagle* staff correspondent on December 14, said, "Wellington citizens are particularly bitter because the agitation which may result in ouster proceedings against the mayor, chief of police and assistant chief, was instigated by 'outsiders.'"[7]

The article went on to recount some of Mayor Thralls' past accomplishments in his position, such as many miles of paved road in town, the memorial auditorium, and the city's clean police record.

The state attorney general filed ouster suits against the mayor and his lawmen on December 22. Two months later, on February 21, 1923, court testimony began. Some witnesses claimed Thralls ignored evidence not only of illegal liquor traffic, but also of prostitution taking place in the city.

In March, headlines read, "Has Mayor Been Double Crossed? – Issue of Ouster is Whether the Police Obeyed His Instructions or Not." The article said the suit closed on March 5th. Mayor Thralls testified in his own defense.

"The mayor gave his testimony in a straightforward manner which convinced everybody in the court room that on matters that he testified to he was telling only the truth," said the article.[8]

Whatever the outcome was to be from this suit, another city election in the first week of April made it irrelevant. Headlines read, "Thralls is Again the City Mayor – Defeats [Ralph] Hangen by 83."[9]

In 1926 Joe Thralls wrote out his will, leaving half of his possessions to his wife, Fannie, and the other half to be divided evenly among his three children.[10] He named his son, Warren, as executor. By then his three children had moved to other places. Josephine (Ellis) lived in Corpus Christi, Texas; Nettie (Endacott) in Roseburg, Oregon; and Warren H. in Wichita, Kansas.

Joe Thralls died in Halstead, Kansas on Wednesday morning, March 14, 1928. He was buried in Prairie Lawn Cemetery in Wellington. The Wellington paper quoted William Allen White, who described Thralls as he knew him late in life.

"No one would suppose from looking at the rugged form and face of the former mayor of the city of Wellington that he has lived long enough to have been a peace officer and terror to evil doers along the border more than half a century ago," he said, "but the fact is that away back in the seventies Joe Thralls had already established a reputation as a hunter of criminals that was known all along the border. Cool, tireless, fearless, and yet never reckless, he had a record of generally getting the men he went after, no matter how desperate they were, or how great the difficulties in the way of the man hunter."[11]

Footnotes

Introduction

[1] G.D. Freeman, *Midnight and Noonday or the Incidental History of Southern Kansas and the Indian Territory, 1871-1890* (Norman: University of Oklahoma Press, 1984, originally published, 1890), 28.

[2] See David Dary, *Cowboy Culture: A Saga of Five Centuries*, (Lawrence: University Press of Kansas, 1981, 1989), 183-190.

[3] John Wesley Hardin, *The Life of John Wesley Hardin as Written by Himself* (Norman: University of Oklahoma, 1961, first published in 1895), 33-50.

[4] *Oxford Times*, July 13, 1871.

[5] Hardin, 49l.

[6] T.A. McNeal, *When Kansas was Young* (Topeka: Capper Publications, Inc., 1940, originally published, 1922), 5.

Chapter 1 - "He said he might spare me $205."

[1] Ray Allen Billington and Martin Ridge, *Westward Expansion: A History of the American Frontier*, 5th Edition (New York: Macmillan Publishing Co., Inc., 1982), 647.

[2] For information on Richard Thralls, see records submitted by Ralph Riggs, 1512 Northridge Drive, Carrollton, Texas, United States of America 75006-1428. These records show Thralls as born on April 23rd, 1753 in Maryland, married to Lucy Milliken on January 3rd, 1788 in Prince Georges County, Maryland, and dying on July 25th, 1835 in Monongalia County, West Virginia. According

to the Craig H. Trout family search site, Isaac Thralls was born on December 31st, 1799, married Elizabeth Ann Johnson, and died on September 5th, 1867.

[3] See the 1870 United States Census for the state of Kansas, Miami County, West Ward Paola (June 4) and 1880 Census, Eudora, Douglas, Kansas (FHL Film 1254380 National Archives Film T9-0380 Page 13C).

[4] *Wellington Monitor-Press*, August 24, 1921, 2.

[5] Ibid.

[6] Ibid.

[7] Ibid.

[8] Ibid.

[9] Ibid.

[10] Ibid.

[11] Ibid., 15.

[12] *Oxford Times*, Saturday, September 30, 1871.

[13] Ibid., Saturday, November 11, 1871.

Chapter 2 - Hackney sets an example

[1] *Oxford Times*, Wednesday, September 25, 1872.

[2] G.D. Freeman, *Midnight and Noonday or the Incidental History of Southern Kansas and the Indian Territory, 1871-1890*, (Norman: University of Oklahoma Press, 1984, originally published, 1890), 121.

[3] *Wellington Monitor-Press*, October 24, 1921.

[4] *Wellington Daily News*, February 11, 1928.

[5] William G. Cutler, *History of the State of Kansas*, (Chicago: A.T. Andreas, 1883), Cowley County, Part 6.

[6] *Wellington Monitor-Press*, October 24, 1921, 14.

[7] Ibid.

[8] Ibid.

[9] Ibid.

[10] See Richard Kay and Mary Ann Wortman's *History of Cowley County Kansas, Volume 1 – The Beginning*, 123-125; 169-176, for

background on Bill Hackney and his involvement in the lynchings in Douglass, Kansas.
[11] *Wellington Monitor-Press*, October 24, 1921, 14.
[12] *Emporia News*, December 16, 1870.
[13] Ibid.
[14] Ibid. For another more detailed account of the Douglass lynchings, see J. Mark Alley, *The Violent Years: The Founding of a Kansas Town* (Hillsboro, Kansas: Prairie Books, 1992).
[15] William G. Cutler, *History of the State of Kansas*, (Chicago: A.T. Andreas, 1883), Sumner County, Part 10.
[16] *Wellington Monitor-Press*, October 24, 1921.

Chapter 3 - "The execution had a salutary effect."

[1] G.D. Freeman, *Midnight and Noonday* (Norman: University of Oklahoma Press, 1984), 37-39.
[2] *Oxford Times*, July 13, 1871.
[3] Ibid., August 3, 1871.
[4] Ibid., September 30, 1871.
[5] Ibid., November 11, 1871.
[6] T.A. McNeal, *When Kansas Was Young* (New York: The MacMillan Company, 1922), 18.
[7] Ibid., 19.
[8] Maria C. McDowell, plaintiff, vs. Hezekiah G. Williams, defendant. Sumner County, 13th district, court case #79A, filed July 22, 1873.
[9] Maria C. McDowell, et. al., plaintiffs, vs. Hezekiah G. Williams, et. al., defendants. Sumner County, 13th district, court case #80A, filed July 24, 1873.
[10] William G. Cutler, *History of the State of Kansas* (Chicago: A.T. Andreas, 1883), Sedgwick County, Part 3.

Chapter 4 - "Bill's language almost made us shudder."

[1] For a fuller account, see *Great Western Indian Fights* by
Members of the Potomac Corral of the Westerners, Chapter 17:
"The Second Battle of Adobe Walls" by J.C. Dykes, (Lincoln:
University of Nebraska Press, 1960).
[2] *The Topeka Commonwealth*, June 24, 1874.
[3] Robert M. Utley, *Frontier Regulars* (Lincoln: University of
Nebraska Press, 1973), 214.
[4] T.A. McNeal, *When Kansas Was Young* (New York: The
McMillan Company, 1922), 17-18.
[5] Ibid., 18.
[6] *The Topeka Daily Commonwealth*, Friday, July 17, 1874.
[7] Ibid.
[8] McNeal, 16. This gun must have been the Sharps New Model
1863 rifle. See David Miller (ed.), *The Illustrated Book of Guns*
(London: Salamander Books, Ltd., 2003), 207.
[9] Ibid., 18.
[10] Ibid.
[11] Ibid., 19.
[12] *Wellington Monitor-Press*, August 24, 1921, 14.
[13] Ibid.
[14] Ibid.
[15] Ibid.

Chapter 5 - "This is the beginning of the end."

[1] *The Wellington Monitor-Press*, August 13, 1924.
[2] *Sumner County Press*, August 6, 1874.
[3] The Colson party, according to the *Sumner County Press*, July
23, 1874, had 16 members. They were the ones who got lost
according to G.D. Freeman (p. 161). But the *Sumner County Press*,
July 30, 1974, in the article, "A Speck of War," said that Sheriff
Davis' party got lost in a sudden cloudburst and bedded down wet
and unsheltered.
[4] *Sumner County Press*, Thursday, September 18, 1873 and
Thursday, November 27, 1873. R.W. Abrell was not alone in

disturbing the peace. The short article said, "I.N. King, W.M. Pryor, O.H. White and R.W. Abrell, all charged with disturbing the peace of the city, were each fined $3.00 and costs. D.W. Jones and J.A. Kirk, who were arraigned on the same charge, were discharged." Jones and Joe Thralls were fellow constables in late 1872. Jones had become Wellington city marshal by 1873. (See *Wellington Banner*, Wednesday, September 25, 1872, *Sumner County Press*, Thursday, September 18 and September 25, 1873).

⁵ Paul I. Wellman, *The Trampling Herd* (Garden City, New York: Doubleday & Co., Inc., 1961, first published, 1939), 185-187.

⁶ T.A. McNeal, *When Kansas was Young* (Topeka: Capper Publications, Inc., 1940, first published, 1922), 48.

⁷ Both G.D. Freeman (*Midnight and Noonday*) and the *Sumner County Press* (July 30, 1874) said that only 10 men remained in the posse after the first two days on the trail though 11 men are mentioned later for a reward. Meers may have been the odd man out since he wasn't mentioned in either account till after the fact.

⁸ This account largely follows the newspaper version of the chase (*Sumner County Press*, July 30, 1874). G.D. Freeman adds other details, mentioning a shootout with buffalo hunters mistaken to be the horse thieves and more twists and turns along the way (*Midnight and Noonday*, chapter 26). How much of his version was true is hard to say, though much of it likely was.

⁹ *Sumner County Press*, July 30, 1874.

¹⁰ Ibid.

¹¹ Ibid., August 13, 1874.

Chapter 6 - "With Judge Lynch on the bench..."

¹ *Sumner County Press*, July 30, 1874.

² See Marianne Deagle, "Kansas' New Death Penalty Law: Will It Be Administered Fairly and Consistently?" *Washburn Law Journal*, Volume 34, Issue 3 (Spring) March 1998, and Genevieve Yost, "History of Lynchings in Kansas" *Kansas State Historical Quarterly*, Volume 2, Number 2, May 1933.

[3] Donald White, *The Border Queen: A History of Early Day Caldwell, Kansas* (Wyandotte, Oklahoma: The Gregath Publishing Company, 1999), 282, quoting from Mrs. J.B. Rideout, *Six Years on the Border* (Philadelphia: Presbyterian Board of Publication, 1883). Mrs. Rideout was wife of Caldwell's first Presbyterian minister, Rev. Jacob B. Rideout.

[4] *Belle Plaine Democrat*, Friday, August 22, 1873.

[5] White, 282-283.

[6] *Sumner County Press*, July 29, 1875 article, "Lynch Law: How a Kansas Mob Hung an Innocent Illinoian."

[7] G.D. Freeman, *Midnight and Noonday* (Norman: University of Oklahoma Press, 1984), 126.

[8] White, 282.

[9] Ibid.

[10] *Sumner County Press*, July 30, 1874.

[11] White, 283.

[12] *Wellington Monitor-Press*, August 24, 1921.

[13] White, 285.

[14] *Wellington Monitor-Press*, August 24, 1921.

[15] Ibid.

[16] White, 284.

[17] *Sumner County Press*, August 6, 1874 article, "The Slate Creek Tragedy."

[18] White, 285.

[19] *Sumner County Press*, August 6, 1874 article, "Truth Stranger Than Fiction."

[20] *Wellington Monitor-Press*, August 24, 1921.

Chapter 7 - "Joe Thralls again did his job."

[1] *Sumner County Press*, Thursday, January 8, 1874.

[2] *Ibid*, Thursday, August 27, 1874.

[3] *Ibid*, Thursday, February 18, 1875.

[4] Glenn Shirley, *Law West of Fort Smith* (Lincoln: University of Nebraska Press, 1957), viii-ix.

[5] *Sumner County Press*, Thursday, May 13, 1875.

[6] *Ibid*, Thursday, February 10, 1881.

[7] Ibid.

[8] *Ibid*, Thursday, November 4, 1880. See also William P. Hackney's article in *Wellington Monitor-Press*, August 24, 1921.

[9] *Sumner County Press*, Thursday, January 11, 1877.

[10] G.D. Freeman, *Midnight and Noonday* (Norman: University of Oklahoma Press, 1984), 163. The United States Marshals Service has emolument returns (payments for services) from U.S. Marshal Benjamin F. Simpson to J.M. Thralls between 1879 and 1885. This shows Thralls was definitely a deputy U.S. marshal during those years. Likely he also served earlier as century old records from the United States Marshals Service are not always complete.

[11] *Sumner County Press*, Thursday, May 3, 1877.

[12] *Sumner County Democrat*, Wednesday, September 19, 1877 article, "Caught at Last."

[13] *Sumner County Press*, Thursday, January 3, 1878; *Sumner County Democrat*, Wednesday, February 6, 1878. Thralls served as city marshal for 16 months. The last issue he was listed as such was in the *Sumner County Press*, Thursday, May 1, 1879.

[14] *Sumner County Press*, Thursday, September 5, 1878.

[15] T.A. McNeal, *When Kansas was Young* (New York: The McMillan Company, 1922), 134-135.

[16] *Sumner County Press*, June 26, 1879 article, "Tardy Retribution!"

[17] McNeal, 136-137.

[18] *Sumner County Press*, Thursday, May 20, 1880.

Chapter 8 - "Sheriff Thralls is entitled to much credit."

[1] *Sumner County Press*, Thursday, September 18, 1879.

[2] Ibid., Thursday, October 30, 1879.

[3] Ibid., Thursday, February 10, 1881.

[4] Ibid., Thursday, January 6, 1881.

[5] *U.S. Census*, June, 1880 for Wellington, Sumner County, Kansas (FHL Film 1254398 National Archives Film T9-0398 Page 278A).

[6] Ibid., June, 1880 for 2nd Ward, Wellington, Sumner County, Kansas (FHL Film 1254398 National Archives Film T9-0398 Page 285B).

[7] Glenn Shirley, *Pawnee Bill: A Biography of Major Gordon W. Lillie* (Lincoln: University of Nebraska Press, 1958), 88.

[8] See the *Caldwell Post*, July 10, 1879 and *Sumner County Press*, July 17, 1879 for the two versions.

[9] *Caldwell Post*, June 24, 1880 article, "The Bullet Does Its Work."

[10] *Caldwell Commercial*, July 1, 1880 article, "The City Government Arrested."

[11] *Caldwell Post*, July 8, 1880.

[12] *Sumner County Press*, Thursday, September 30, 1880 article, "Arrest of Dave Sprague."

[13] *Caldwell Post*, September 16, 1880.

[14] Ibid., October 14, 1880.

[15] *Sumner County Press*, Thursday, November 4, 1880.

Chapter 9 - "His re-election is foreordained."

[1] *Sumner County Press*, Thursday, March 24, 1881.

[2] Ibid., Thursday, May 5, 1881 and January 5, 1882.

[3] Ibid., Thursday, May 19, 1881.

[4] Ibid., Thursday, August 25, 1881.

[5] G.D. Freeman, *Midnight and Noonday* (Norman: University of Oklahoma Press, 1984), 203.

[6] *Arkansas City Traveler,* August 31, 1881, quoting from the *Wellington Wellingtonian.*

[7] *Sumner County Press*, Thursday, September 15, 1881.

[8] Ibid., Thursday, September 29, 1881.

Chapter 10 - A Great Reputation Captured

¹ *Sumner County Press*, Thursday, October 27, 1881.
² Ibid., Thursday, November 10, 1881.
³ Ibid., Thursday, December 1, 1881 and *Cowley County Courant,* December 8, 1881.
⁴ See *Caldwell Post* and *Sumner County Press*, December 22, 1881, and G.D Freeman, *Midnight and Noonday* (Norman: University of Oklahoma Press, 1984), 250-267, for more details.
⁵ In a post card from Mrs. Campbell to her mother-in-law dated December 21, 1881, Mrs. Campbell said she found 27 bullet holes in Campbell's clothes. He had a book and a rolled up newspaper in his vest pocket when he was shot. One bullet went through the book and into the newspaper and stopped before entering his body, according to Mrs. Campbell. (See "W.E. Campbell, Pioneer Kansas Livestockman," by C.W. Campbell, *Kansas Historical Quarterly*, August, 1948, Vol. XVI, No. 3).
⁶ *Caldwell Commercial*, Thursday, January 19, 1882.
⁷ *Wellington Wellingtonian*, Thursday, January 19, 1882.

Chapter 11 - "I'm Thralls and I want you."

¹ *Caldwell Commercial*, June 29, 1882.
² Nyle H. Miller and Joseph W. Snell, *Why the West Was Wild* (Topeka: Kansas State Historical Society, 1963), 57-63, and G.D. Freeman, *Midnight and Noonday* (Norman: University of Oklahoma Press, 1984), 207-209.
³ *Caldwell Commercial*, July 13, 1882.
⁴ Miller and Snell, 66.
⁵ Ibid., 60.
⁶ *Winfield Courier,* September 21, 1882.
⁷ Nyle H. Miller and Joseph W. Snell, *Great Gunfighters of the Kansas Cowtowns: 1867-1886* (Lincoln: University of Nebraska Press, 1967), 48.
⁸ *Winfield Courier* and *Caldwell Commercial*, October 12, 1882.

[9] *Winfield Courier*, October 26, and *Caldwell Post*, October 19 and October 26, 1882.
[10] Miller and Snell, 66.
[11] *Caldwell Commercial* and *Sumner County Press*, Thursday, November 16, 1882.
[12] *Caldwell Post*, January 4, 1883.

Chapter 12 - Friendship as strong as brotherhood

[1] *Winfield Courier*, Thursday, May 1, 1873.
[2] Ibid., Thursday, May 22, 1874.
[3] Ibid., Thursday, July 11, 1875; June 1, June22, July 6, and July 20, 1876.
[4] Ibid., Thursday, August 22, 1877.
[5] Ibid., Thursday, September 6, 1877.
[6] Ibid., Thursday, September 13, 1877 and *Arkansas City Traveler*, September 26, 1877.
[7] *Winfield Courier*, Thursday, April 25, 1878 and May 1, 1879.
[8] Ibid., Thursday, May 29, 1879.
[9] Ibid., Thursday, June 5, 1879.
[10] *Arkansas City Traveler*, July 23, 1879.
[11] *Winfield Courier*, September 11, 1879 and *Arkansas City Traveler*, September 10, 1879.
[12] Ibid., November 20 and December 6, 1879.
[13] Ibid., January 1 and February 12, 1880.
[14] Ibid., June 2, 1881.
[15] Ibid., June 30, 1881.
[16] Ibid., July 28, 1881.
[17] *Arkansas City Traveler*, October 19, 1881.
[18] *Winfield Courier*, October 20, 1881.
[19] Ibid., January 25, 1883.
[20] Cutler's *History of the State of Kansas* said Jacobus told Shenneman of the suspicious boarder. But the current local newspapers all reported the school teacher told Shenneman.

[21] *Winfield Courier*, January 18 and January 25, 1883, and William G. Cutler, *History of the State of Kansas* (Chicago: A.T. Andreas, 1883), Cowley County, Part 13.

[22] *Winfield Courier*, February 8, 1883.

[23] Ibid., February 1, 1883.

[24] Ibid.

[25] Ibid., February 8, 1883.

Chapter 13 - "We have no enmity."

[1] *Caldwell Commercial*, Thursday, February 15, 1883.

[2] *Winfield Courier*, April 19, 1883 and *Caldwell Commercial*, April 12, 1883.

[3] *Caldwell Journal*, August 16, 1883.

[4] *Sumner County Press*, August 16, 1883. The eight cowboys listed in the *Caldwell Journal*, August 16, 1883 were Bob Mitchell, A. T. Mitchell, J. W. Gwinn, Harry Halsell, J. F. McClosky [McClusky], T. A. Standard, Dick Weston, and Powell Wood. The *Arkansas City Traveler*, August 22, 1883 listed them as Bob Mitchell, A. T. Mitchell, J. W. Guinn, Harry Halsell, J. F. McClusky [McClosky], T. A. Standard, Dick Weston, and Powell Wood

[5] *Sumner County Press*, August 23, 1883.

[6] Ibid.

[7] *Caldwell Journal*, August 16, 1883.

[8] *Arkansas City Traveler*, August 22, 1883.

[9] *Wellington Wellingtonian*, August 30, 1883.

[10] *Sumner County Press*, September 6, 1883 article, "The Sheriff's Office."

[11] Ibid., September 13, 1883 article "A Flimsy Defense."

[12] *Caldwell Journal*, October 4, 1883.

[13] Ibid., November 22, 1883.

Chapter 14 - Civilian Leader

[1] *Caldwell Journal*, November 22, 1883.

[2] Sumner County, Kansas, Probate Court Case # 6378.

[3] *Wellington Monitor-Press*, March 15, 1928.

[4] Ibid., September 6, 1922.

[5] Ibid., November 22, 1922.

[6] *Chronicles of Oklahoma*, Volume 6, No. 2, June 1928, 251.
Joe Thralls was among other members who would make a name for themselves. Among them were authors William E. Connelley and Frank Dobie.

[7] *Wellington Monitor-Press*, December 20, 1922.

[8] Ibid., March 7, 1923.

[9] Ibid., April 4, 1923.

[10] Last Will and Testament of J.M. Thralls, Sumner County, Kansas, Probate Court Case # 6378.

[11] *Wellington Monitor-Press*, Thursday, March 15, 1928.

Bibliography

Adams, Andy. *The Log of a Cowboy.* Lincoln: University of Nebraska Press, 1903, 1964.

Alley, J. Mark. *The Violent Years: The Founding of a Kansas Town.* Hillsboro, Kansas: Prairie Books, 1992.

Bader, Robert Smith. *Prohibition in Kansas: A History.* Lawrence: University Press of Kansas, 1986.

Barnard, Edward S., ed. *Story of the Great American West.* Pleasantville, New York: The Reader's Digest Association, Inc., 1977.

Barra, Allen. *Inventing Wyatt Earp: His Life and Many Legends.* New York: Carroll & Graf Publishers, Inc., 1998.

Bergon, Frank, and Zeese Papanikolas, eds. *Looking Far West: The Search for the American West in History, Myth, and Literature.* New York: The New American Library, 1978.

Billington, Ray Allen. *America's Frontier Heritage.* Albuquerque: University of New Mexico Press, 1974, 1963.

_____. *The Westward Movement in the United States.* New York: D. Van Nostrand Co., 1959.

Blackburn, Forrest R., and others, eds. *Kansas and the West: Bicentennial Essays in Honor of Nyle H. Miller.* Topeka: Kansas State Historical Society, 1976.

Bogue, Allan G., Thomas D. Phillips, and James E. Wright, eds. *The West of the American People.* Itasca, Illinois: F.E. Peacock Publishers, Inc., 1970.

Brash, Sarah, ed. *The American Story: Settling the West.* Richmond, Virginia: Time Life, Inc., 1996.

Breakenridge, William M. *Helldorado.* Lincoln: University of Nebraska Press, 1928, 1992.

Breihan, Carl W. *Great Lawmen of the West.* New York: Bonanza Books, 1963.

Bright, John D., ed. *Kansas: The First Century.* Volume 1. New York: Lewis Historical Publishing Company, 1956.

Brown, Dee. *The American West.* New York: Simon & Schuster, 1994.

Brown, Dee, with Martin F. Schmitt. *Trail Driving Days.* New York: Charles Scribner's Sons, 1952.

Burns, Walter Noble. *The Saga of Billy the Kid.* New York: Doubleday & Company, 1925, 1926.

Cain, Del. *Lawmen of the Old West: The Good Guys.* Plano, Texas: Republic of Texas Press, 2000.

Calhoun, Frederick S. *The Lawmen: United States Marshals and their Deputies, 1789-1989.* Washington, D.C.: Smithsonian Institution Press, 1989.

Chrisman, Harry E. *1001 Most-Asked Questions About the American West.* Athens, Ohio: Swallow Press Books, Ohio University Press, 1982.

Coke, Tom S. *Old West Justice in Belle Plaine, Kansas.* Bowie, Maryland: Heritage Books, Inc., 2002.

Colbert, David, ed. *Eyewitness to the American West: From the Aztec Empire to the Digital Frontier in the Words of Those Who Saw It Happen.* New York: Viking Press, 1998.

Cook, Rod. *George and Maggie and the Red Light Saloon.* New York: iUniverse, Inc., 2003.

Crutchfield, James A., Bill O'Neal, and Dale L. Walker. *Legends of the Wild West.* Lincolnwood, Illinois: Publications International, Ltd., 1995.

Cunningham, Eugene. *Triggernometry: A Gallery of Gunfighters.* Norman: University of Oklahoma Press, 1996, originally published, 1934.

Dary, David. *The Buffalo Book: The Saga of an American Symbol.* New York: Avon Books, 1974.

_____. *Cowboy Culture: A Saga of Five Centuries.* Lawrence: University of Kansas Press, 1981, 1989.

Drago, Harry Sinclair, and Richard Patterson. *Outlaws on Horseback.* Lincoln: University of Nebraska Press, 1964, 1998.
_____. *Road Agents and Train Robbers: Half a Century of Western Banditry.* New York: Dodd, Mead & Co., 1973.
Dykstra, Robert R. *The Cattle Towns.* Lincoln: University of Nebraska Press, 1968, 1983.
Einsel, Mary. *Stagecoach West to Kansas: True Stories of the Kansas Plains.* Boulder, Colorado: Pruett Publishing Company, 1970.
Erdoes, Richard R. *Saloons of the Old West.* Avenel, New Jersey: Gramercy Books, 1997, 1979.
Erwin, Richard E. *The Truth About Wyatt Earp.* Carpinteria, CA: The O.K. Press, 1992.
An Eye-Witness. *The Dalton Brothers and Their Astounding Career of Crime.* Chicago: Laird & Lee, December 1892. Reproduced by Jingle Bob/Crown Publishers, Inc., New York, 1977
Etulain, Richard W. & Glenda Riley, eds. *With Badges and Bullets: Lawmen & Outlaws in the Old West.* Golden, Colorado: Fulcrum Publishing, 1999.
Federal Writer's Project of the Work Projects Administration for the State of Kansas. *The WPA Guide to 1930's Kansas.* Lawrence: University Press of Kansas, 1939, 1984.
Fitzgerald, Daniel. *Ghost Towns of Kansas: A Traveler's Guide.* Lawrence: University Press of Kansas, 1988.
Flaherty, Thomas H., ed. *The Wild West.* New York: Time Warner Co., 1993.
Flanagan, Mike. *The Complete Idiot's Guide to The Old West.* New York: Alpha Books, 1999.
Foner, Eric. *A Short History of Reconstruction, 1863-1877.* New York: Harper & Row, Publishers, Inc., 1990.
Forbis, William H. *The Cowboys.* New York: Time-Life Books, Inc., 1973.
Freeman, G.D. *Midnight and Noonday or the Incidental History of Southern Kansas and the Indian Territory, 1871-1890.* Norman:

University of Oklahoma Press, 1984 (Edited with an Introduction and Notes, by Richard L. Lane), originally published, 1890.

Gard, Wayne. *The Chisholm Trail.* Norman: University of Oklahoma Press, 1954.

_____. *Frontier Justice.* Norman: University of Oklahoma Press, 1949.

_____. *The Great Buffalo Hunt: Its history and drama, and its role in the opening of the West.* Lincoln: University of Nebraska Press, 1959.

Garrett, Pat F. *The Authentic Life of Billy the Kid.* Norman: University of Oklahoma Press (New Edition), 1954. (Originally published in 1882).

Hardin, John Wesley. *The Life of John Wesley Hardin as Written by Himself.* Norman: University of Oklahoma Press, 1961.

Harman, Samuel W. *Hell on the Border.* Lincoln: University of Nebraska Press, 1898, 1992.

Hine, Robert V. *The American West: An Interpretive History.* Boston: Little, Brown and Company, 1973

Horan, James D. *Desperate Men.* Lincoln: University of Nebraska Press, 1949, 1962, 1997.

_____. *The Gunfighters: The Authentic Wild West.* New York: Gramercy Books, 1976, 1994.

_____. *The Lawmen: The Authentic Wild West.* New York: Gramercy Books, 1980, 1996.

_____. *The Outlaws: The Authentic Wild West.* New York: Gramercy Books, Books, 1977, 1995.

Hough, Emerson. *The Passing of the Frontier: A Chronicle of the Old West.* New Haven: Yale University Press, 1918.

Ise, John. *Sod and Stubble: The Story of a Kansas Homestead.* Lincoln: University of Nebraska Press, 1936, 1967.

Johnson, Dorothy M. *Western Badmen.* New York: Dodd, Mead & Company, 1970, 1972.

Kansas Atlas & Gazetteer. Yarmouth, Maine: DeLorme, 1997.

Kay, Richard and Mary Ann Wortman. *History of Cowley County Kansas, Volume 1 – The Beginning.* Arkansas City, Kansas: Arkansas City Historical Society, 1996.

Kelly, Charles. *The Outlaw Trail: A History of Butch Cassidy and the Wild Bunch.* Lincoln: University of Nebraska Press, 1938, 1959.

Lake, Carolyn, ed. *Undercover for Wells Fargo: The Unvarnished Recollections of Fred Dodge.* New York: Houghton Mifflin Company, 1969, 1973.

Lake, Stuart N. *Wyatt Earp: Frontier Marshal.* Boston: Houghton Mifflin, 1931.

Lamar, Howard Roberts, ed. *The New Encyclopedia of the American West.* New Haven & London: Yale University Press, 1998, 1977.

Lewis, Jon E. *The Mammoth Book of the West.* New York: Carroll & Graf Publishers, Inc., 1996.

Locke, Raymond Friday, ed. *The American West.* Los Angeles: Mankind Publishing Company, 1971.

Long, R. M. "Dick". *Wichita Century: A Pictorial History of Wichita, Kansas, 1870-1970.* Wichita: The Wichita Historical Museum Association, Inc., 1969.

McCoy, Joseph G. *Historic Sketches of the Cattle Trade of the West and Southwest.* Kansas City: Ramsey, Millett & Hudson, 1874.

McLoughlin, Denis. *Wild and Woolly: An Encyclopedia of the Old West.* New York: Barnes & Noble, Inc., 1975, 1996.

McNeal, T.Λ. *When Kansas Was Young.* New York: MacMillan Company, 1922.

Marks, Paula Mitchell. *And Die in the West: The Story of the OK Corral Gunfight.* Norman: University of Oklahoma Press, 1996.

Merk, Frederick. *History of the Westward Movement.* New York: Alfred A. Knopf, Inc., 1978.

Metz, Leon Claire. *The Shooters.* New York: Berkley Books, 1976, 1996.

_____. *John Wesley Hardin: Dark Angel of Texas.* Norman: University of Oklahoma Press, 1996.

Miller, David (ed.). *The Illustrated Book of Guns.* London: Salamander Books Ltd., 2003.

Miller, Floyd. *Bill Tilghman: The Biography of a Lawman.* New York: Curtis Books, 1967, 1968.

Miller, Nyle H., and Joseph W. Snell. *Great Gunfighters of the Kansas Cowtowns, 1867-1886.* Lincoln: University of Nebraska Press, 1963.

_____. *Why the West was Wild: A Contemporary Look at the Antics of Some Highly Publicized Kansas Cowtown Personalities.* Topeka: Kansas State Historical Society, 1963.

Milner, Clyde A., Carol A. O'Connor, and others, eds. *The Oxford History of the American West.* New York: Oxford University Press, 1994.

Miner, Craig. *Kansas: The History of the Sunflower State, 1854-2000.* Lawrence: University Press of Kansas, 2002.

_____. *West of Wichita: Settling the High Plains of Kansas, 1865-1890.* Lawrence: University Press of Kansas, 1986.

_____. *Wichita: The Early Years, 1865-1880.* Lincoln: University of Nebraska Press, 1989.

_____. *Wichita: The Magic City: An Illustrated History.* Wichita, Kansas: Wichita-Sedgwick County Historical Museum Association, 1989.

Monaghan, Jay, (ed.). *The Book of the American West.* New York: Bonanza Books, 1963.

Myers, John Myers. *Bravos of the West.* Lincoln: University of Nebraska Press, 1962, 1990.

_____. *Tombstone's Early Years.* Lincoln: University of Nebraska Press, 1950.

Nix, Evett Dumas, as told to Gordon Hines. *Oklahombres: Particularly the Wilder Ones.* Lincoln: University of Nebraska Press, 1929, 1993.

Oklahoma Atlas & Gazetteer. Yarmouth, Maine: DeLorme, 1998.

O'Neal, Bill. *Caldwell in the 1870's and 1880's: The Rowdy Years of the Border Queen.* Privately published, date unknown.

_____. *Encyclopedia of Western Gunfighters.* Norman: University of Oklahoma Press, 1979.

_____. *Henry Brown: The Outlaw-Marshal.* College Station, Texas: Creative Publishing Company, Early West Series, 1980.

_____. *Historic Ranches of the Old West.* Austin, Texas: Eakin Press, 1997.

Phillips, Charles. *Heritage of the West.* New York: Crescent Books, 1992.

Prassel, Frank Richard. *The Western Peace Officer: A Legacy of Law and Order.* Norman: University of Oklahoma Press, 1972.

Preston, Ralph & Monte. *Early Kansas: An Historical Atlas.* Tidewater, Oregon: Pioneer Press, 1997.

Rabinowitz, Harold. *Black Hats and White Hats: Heroes and Villains of the West.* New York: Metro Books, 1996.

Richmond, Robert W. *Kansas: A Land of Contrasts.* St. Louis, Missouri: Forum Press, 1974, 1980.

Richmond, Robert W., and Robert W. Mardock, eds. *A Nation Moving West: Readings in the History of the American Frontier.* Lincoln: University of Nebraska Press, 1966.

Roosevelt, Theodore. *Ranch Life and the Hunting-Trail.* New York: The Century Company, 1888, 1896.

Rosa, Joseph G. *The Gunfighter: Man or Myth?* Norman: University of Oklahoma Press, 1969.

_____. *They Called Him Wild Bill: The Life and Adventures of James Butler Hickok.* Norman: University of Oklahoma Press, 1964.

_____. *The West of Wild Bill Hickok.* Norman: University of Oklahoma Press, 1994.

Ruede, Howard, Edited by John Ise. *Sod-House Day: Letters from a Kansas Homesteader, 1877-78.* Lawrence: University Press of Kansas, 1937, 1965, 1983.

Shirley, Glenn. *Bell Starr and Her Times: The Literature, the Facts, and the Legends.* Norman: University of Oklahoma Press, 1990.

_____. *Law West of Fort Smith.* Lincoln: University of Nebraska Press, 1957, 1986.

_____. *Pawnee Bill: A Biography of Major Gordon W. Lillie.* Lincoln: University of Nebraska Press, 1958.

Siringo, Charles A. *A Texas Cowboy.* Lincoln: University of Nebraska Press, 1950, 1979, originally published, 1886.

Smith, Henry Nash. *Virgin Land: The American West as Symbol and Myth.* New York: Vintage Books, 1959.

Tefertiller, Casey. *Wyatt Earp: The Life Behind the Legend.* New York: John Wiley & Sons, Inc., 1997.

Texas Atlas & Gazetteer. Yarmouth, Maine: DeLorme, 2001.

Trachtman, Paul. *The Gunfighters.* Alexandria, Virginia: Time-Life Books, Inc., 1974.

Turner, Frederick Jackson. *Frontier and Section.* Englewood Cliffs, New Jersey: Prentice-Hall, Inc., 1961.

Utley, Robert. *Billy the Kid: A Short and Violent Life.* Lincoln: University of Nebraska Press, 1989.

Vestal, Stanley. *Dodge City: Queen of Cowtowns.* Lincoln: University of Nebraska Press, 1952, 1972, 1998.

Webb, Walter Prescott. *The Great Plains.* New York: Grosset & Dunlap, 1931, 1971.

Wellman, Paul I. *A Dynasty of Western Outlaws.* New York: Doubleday, 1961.

_____. *The Trampling Herd: The Story of the Cattle Range in America.* Garden City, New York: Doubleday & Company, Inc., 1961, originally published, 1939.

White, Donald. *The Border Queen: A History of Early Day Caldwell, Kansas.* Wyandotte, Oklahoma: The Gregath Publishing Company, 1999.

Wood, L. Curtise. *Dynamics of Faith: Wichita 1870-1897.* Wichita, Kansas: Wichita State University, 1969.

Writer's Program of the Work Projects Administration in the State of Oklahoma. *The WPA Guide to 1930's Oklahoma.* Lawrence: University Press of Kansas, 1941, 1986.

Yeatman, Ted P. *Frank and Jesse James: The Story Behind the Legend.* Nashville: Cumberland Publishing, Inc., 2000.

Yost, Nellie Snyder. *Medicine Lodge: The Story of a Kansas Frontier Town.* Chicago: The Swallow Press, Inc., 1970.

Young, Fredric R. *Dodge City: Up Through a Century in Story and Pictures.* Dodge City: Boot Hill Museum, Inc., 1972.

Index

107, 108, 111, 112, 115,
116, 117, 118, 120, 121,
122, 123, 124, 125, 127,
128, 130, 131, 133, 135,
147, 148, 150, 152, 158,
165, 175, 176
Calkins, Judson H. "Judd",
66, 69, 70, 71, 72
Campbell, Wilbur Campbell,
84, 124
Carr, Marshal B.P. "Bat",
130
Carson, Christopher "Kit", 44
Chamberlin, W.E., 31
Cheyenne-Arapaho Agency,
49
Chikaskia River, 30, 35, 55,
59, 60, 150
Chisholm Trail, 2, 3, 4, 5,
30, 34, 37, 40, 59, 79,
98, 140, 162, 172
Clearwater, Kansas, 4, 69
Clements brothers, 4
Cobb, Charles, 140, 141,
142, 143, 144, 145, 146,
147
Cohron, 5
Coke, Gov. Richard, 83, 170
Colder, Sadie, 117
Cole, 111, 112
Colson, A.M., 59, 60, 62, 63

Corbin, Jack "California Joe",
23, 24, 25, 29
Cowley County, 32, 97, 99,
129, 135, 136, 137, 139,
140, 143, 144, 146, 173
Crats, "Dutch" Fred, 34
Crawford, 24
Cummins, Scott, 14

Danford, J.S., 120, 121
Davis, R.A., 15, 20, 37, 39,
50, 59, 60, 62, 63, 64,
65, 66, 70, 71, 73, 74,
76, 81, 82, 115, 116,
147, 148, 158, 159
Devore, H.J., 60, 62
Dixon, Billy, 44, 45, 46, 59,
103
Dodge City, Kansas, 2, 3, 5,
7, 43, 44, 45, 51, 61, 67,
68, 79, 99, 100, 115,
176, 177
Doncarlos, W.C., 67
Douglass, Kansas, 23, 24,
25, 26, 28, 29, 143, 144
Drea, Mike, 25
Drumm, Major Andrew, 59,
60
Drummond, Bob, 59

Riley, T.J., 51, 80, 171
Roberts, Lizzie, 111, 112, 115, 116, 173
Rodgers, Jim, 5

Segerman, Louis, 104
Seguin, Texas, 83
Shadler brothers, 46
Sharps Rifle, 46, 51, 53, 58
Shawver, C.C., 97
Shearman, 14, 15, 16, 19, 84, 150
Shenneman, Albert, 8, 80, 129, 130, 135, 136, 137, 138, 139, 140, 141, 142, 143, 144, 145
Sheridan, General Philip, 49
Sherman, Major General William, 49, 51, 121
Shoo Fly Creek, 16, 34
Slate Creek, 5, 14, 30, 36, 41, 54, 63, 73, 74, 75
Smith, Vann, 19, 23, 24, 25, 29, 34, 35, 36, 54, 66, 69, 71, 72, 73, 75, 76, 86, 87, 88, 93, 97, 99, 103, 116, 120, 121, 131, 140, 141, 143, 169, 176
Southwestern Stage Company, 58
Spear, Charles L., 104, 105, 108, 121, 123

St. John, Gov. John P., 97, 128, 129, 132
Starlight, Jake, 34
Stevenson, R.W., 59, 97
Stipp, James, 51
Sumner City, Kansas, 5, 30, 34
Sumner County, 2, 3, 4, 5, 6, 15, 19, 20, 30, 33, 36, 58, 72, 73, 79, 81, 82, 85, 93, 94, 95, 97, 98, 99, 100, 102, 114, 115, 119, 128, 135, 146, 149, 151, 154, 155, 156, 157, 158, 159, 161, 162, 163, 165
Sumner County Press, 73
Sun City, Kansas, 48

Talbot, Jim, 121, 122, 123, 125, 129, 130, 134
Terrill, Dave, 66, 69, 70, 71, 72
Texas Rangers, 110
Thralls, Elzy, 6, 12, 13, 14, 15, 16, 55, 80, 97, 110, 133, 134, 148, 149, 150, 151, 154, 155, 156, 158, 159, 161, 162
Thralls, Joseph M., 1, 2, 3, 5, 6, 7, 8, 9, 11, 12, 13, 15, 16, 19, 20, 21, 29, 32,

Williamson, L.T., 57, 59, 62, 63, 64
Wilsie, C., 67
Wilson, John, 83, 101, 102, 109, 122, 123, 136

Wood, P.A., 13, 15, 19, 85, 101, 102, 151, 176
Woodman, W.C., 15, 16, 138
Woods, George, 115, 116, 147, 150, 158

www.ingramcontent.com/pod-product-compliance
Lightning Source LLC
Chambersburg PA
CBHW061734270326
41928CB00011B/2228